CURATING INQUIRIES

CURATING INQUIRIES

Curriculum Design and Mapping for Primary Schools

GRANT LEWIS

To Belinda, Issy, Emile and Amelie,

"All it takes is one decision. A lot of guts, a little vision"
– **Placebo: 'Slave to the Wage'**

ACKNOWLEDGEMENTS

*"'Cause I only have one second, this minute today.
I can't press rewind and turn it back and call it now"*
– **Katie Noonan: 'Breathe in Now'**

Writing this book, *Curating Inquiries*, would not have been possible without the unwavering and incredible support of my gorgeous wife, Belinda. She had long told me that I should write a book as I had all these ideas and thoughts bouncing around. Without her, none of anything I've achieved as an adult would have been possible. Her selfless support and encouragement have been a constant source of inspiration and magic.

My three beautiful children, Issy, Emile and Amelie, have checked in and asked so many times how my book was going. Their expressed pride in their dad writing has fuelled my desire to keep going. But it is their smiles and daily love that means the world.

To my family and friends who have supported me and cheered from the sidelines, it has been fantastic to have your support.

To Alicia Cohen from Amba Press, who took a punt on a discovery call with me and saw something in me that I wasn't sure I had. Thank you for giving me the opportunity to turn my thoughts into words and into this book.

To Richard Gerver, who graciously and generously offered to read and review the book prior to publishing. Your constant source of encouragement and affirmations are truly humbling.

To Sandy Skeehan and Melissa Alexander, who also took the opportunity to read prior to publishing. Your insights and feedback were taken on board and considered. They helped shape and frame the final version.

To all the incredible teachers I've had the pleasure of working with and I've learnt from.

To the students I've taught or been in schools with, you are the reason we try to get better at what we do. You are our collective 'why'.

Copyright © Grant Lewis 2023

All rights reserved. No part of this book may be reproduced or transmitted in any form or by any means, electronic or mechanical, including photocopying, recording or by any information storage and retrieval system, without prior permission in writing from the publisher.

Published by Amba Press
Melbourne, Australia
www.ambapress.com.au

Editor – Rica Dearman
Cover Designer – Tess McCabe

ISBN: 9781922607904 (pbk)
ISBN: 9781922607911 (ebk)

A catalogue record for this book is available from the National Library of Australia.

CONTENTS

Introduction		1
Chapter 1	Inquiry is messy – but what is it?	5
Chapter 2	Conceptual framework	19
Chapter 3	Mapping curriculum	31
Chapter 4	Framing the inquiries	49
Chapter 5	Starting with a question is questionable	63
Chapter 6	Breaking it down into smaller parts	77
Chapter 7	Mapping the year	91
Chapter 8	Assessing the learning	107
Chapter 9	Provocations	125
Chapter 10	Honouring student voice	139
Chapter 11	Lights, camera, ~~teacher-led~~ action	155
Conclusion	Final thoughts	169
References		171
About the author		175

SPOTIFY PLAYLIST

For those who want to 'sing along' with the book, I've created a playlist on Spotify. Feel free to visit and listen – or sing along!

INTRODUCTION

*"The mediocre teacher tells. The good teacher explains.
The superior teacher demonstrates. The great teacher inspires"*
– **William A Ward (1968)**

*"Do you recall the things that used to give us joy?
When our imaginations could take us anywhere"*
– **Ásgeir: 'Youth'**

Education systems articulate standards for teachers to aspire to, meet or exceed. Whether it is:

- *AITSL standards (2017):* "The Australian Professional Standards for Teachers help you understand and develop your teaching practice and expertise across 4 career stages. By demonstrating the Standards you can have maximum impact on all learners."
- *Teachers' Standards from the United Kingdom (2011):* "Teachers make the education of their pupils their first concern, and are accountable for achieving the highest possible standards in work and conduct."
- *National Board for Professional Teaching Standards from the United States of America (1989):* "Proposition 1: Teachers are committed to students and their learning".
- *National Curriculum Frameworks for Teacher Education from India (2010)*, with an explicit focus "to bring about a paradigm shift in education with focus on holistic development of children, emphasis on skilling, vital role of teachers, learning in mother tongue, cultural rootedness".
- *UNESCO* (2019), with the aim to develop "professional teaching standards aims to improve teacher quality, teaching and learning".

No matter the country or governing body, there are standards that teachers are required to meet. Some express minimum benchmarks, others are aspirational. But all exist to create learning opportunities for our students.

Or, put in the words of the sustainable development goals from UNESCO SDG4, "Ensure inclusive and equitable quality education and promote lifelong learning opportunities for all."

What makes a good teacher? Indeed, what makes a great teacher? The answer is complex and challenging to articulate. Different jurisdictions, governing/regulatory bodies articulate similar concepts in differing ways. Some things that great teachers do are tricky to measure; there are nuances, micro expressions, constant adjusting and ultimately connections and relationships unique and ever evolving. Removing all curriculum and pedagogical knowledge, there are behaviours and approaches that great teachers exhibit.

Before children, my wife and I, along with our Thursday pizza crew, would, every week, go for pizza at the same restaurant. Initially, the arrangements went from making a booking and leaving our name, time, phone number and number of guests. As customers we read the menu, made some choices and tried different things – no sharing, just individual meals. After a few weeks and months, it moved to having a booking and recognising our voice and it was a question of how many. The time was known. We were getting into familiar grooves with orders and there was a common understanding that we would have the same entrée to share.

After more time, it evolved to getting a preferred table, the same night, same time, and they would move chairs and tables around to adjust to our numbers. We started to have usual meals and some of the waiting staff remembered or got close to our individual orders. We even started to chat to people at tables near us, as they were regulars, too.

Ultimately, there was a reserved table each week and our entrée would be waiting on the table for us. No need to order the food – they would simply know what to cook based on who had arrived. And sure enough, each week they nailed it: such great customer service.

But was that because they knew from repetition? Or was it something deeper? I'd like to think that the human experience allows us to have that something deeper, a connection, a relationship or bond.

If we can experience this level of service or relationship in a setting like this, imagine what we can do in schools.

Every day, we have the same people coming into our schools and classrooms, and each day is an opportunity to make a positive difference in their lives. We are charged with the responsibility of caring for these students and supporting their learning as students and as people.

The ideas covered in this book are offerings and considerations for you. It is not to develop this as a templated, cookie-cutter approach that you can apply to your setting. There is no singular silver bullet for the ills of education or of our profession. Students are different, they learn differently. Teachers are different, they teach differently. Schools are different, they school (educate) differently.

My aim in writing this book isn't to provide all the answers or solutions (as no one has them), moreover, it is to provide pathways, options and considerations for you. Perhaps some things you read resonate and affirm your thinking, or perhaps they are new to you and you can adopt them. Whichever is your reality, my hope is that in reading this book, you take away something practical that you can apply to your context.

Ultimately, we all got into teaching to make a difference to the lives of students. I've yet to meet a teacher who had a different plan initially. In doing what we do, in the systems and schools we are in, we can lose sight of the big picture – the students. It seems as though we spend so much time documenting, writing up incident reports, completing the ever-increasing required documentation that we could all do with an administrative assistant. Sadly, that is not, and most likely never will be, our reality. 'Administrivia', a term coined by Harlen Fiske Stone (1923), captures the frustrations of teachers with 'paperwork'. Administrivia is the mundane tasks that do not directly relate to the primary purpose of our work.

This book is aimed to set teachers up for success and have as many 'big things' planned before the next year begins and think about some of the ways in which to engage with inquiries and involve student voice and genuine action. In developing a yearly plan in advance, it liberates so much headspace and anxiety or pressure. Knowing where you are going takes care of "What am I going to teach?" and provides space for the more important "How am I going to explore this with my students?" It doesn't ignore "What do my students want to learn?" if you ask those questions in advance, then plan in response.

There are lots of different incarnations or versions of inquiry-based learning that exist, and all come back to students asking and answering questions. Through the frameworks and processes offered in this book, my hope is to support teachers to have structures around them to enable them to achieve success in setting up the memorable, powerful and engaging learning experiences for their students.

This book explores what inquiry is, how to make sense of it all and still remain accountable to curriculum and student voice. It supports teachers or schools to develop a conceptual framework in which to scaffold the learning around while in the process of developing inquiries worth learning about. From looking at how to map curriculum across a year (or more than one year) across the framework, it is designed to be practical and provide strategies and protocols to be applied in a primary school setting.

Time is spent in developing statements that require students to inquire into them, rather than answer questions from teachers. The aim is to design learning that engages students and honours the accountabilities we have in the day-to-day reality of teaching. This is not a book that is pure inquiry when students are in total control of their learning, it is a book that supports teachers to develop more knowledge around planning for an inquiry and providing the time and space for students to grow in their confidence and skills in inquiry. I toyed with the idea of having the book in two parts, one where the setting up is part one and part two the application in the classroom, but they blur too much. What we do in planning directly impacts on the classroom and I couldn't meaningfully separate them with fidelity.

Throughout this book, it will reference teachers as such, but I actually prefer the term 'educator'. Purely from the etymology of the word: *educere* is the root word for education (or *ex* + *ducere*), which literally means to lead out. The notion of teachers as the ones to lead out, toward the light, toward a new beginning, toward a future, is one I love and wholeheartedly embrace. A teacher's job, as we all well know, is not limited to teaching. We educate. We lead others out. We lead others. We lead.

Each chapter of this book begins with two quotes, one that is purely academic or thematic from a credible voice that has been quoted in many different instances. The others are quotes from songs. They so happen to be songs that I know and love, but the message in the songs capture the essence of what each chapter is about. It is either done analogously or through interpretation on the reader's behalf. But each is placed there deliberately to orient you, the reader. Some of you may sing the tune in your head upon recognition, others may check out the song and never listen to it again, but the intention behind it is to provoke your thinking.

My hope is that you are a great teacher (educator), and that through reading this book, you continue on your journey to greatness and inspire others in this wonderful profession of ours.

CHAPTER 1

INQUIRY IS MESSY – BUT WHAT IS IT?

"The principle goal of education is to create men and women who are capable of doing new things, not simply repeating what other generations have done"
– **Jean Piaget (attributed)**

"Reminding of this mess we're in"
– **PJ Harvey & Thom Yorke: 'This Mess We're In'**

What is ice?

Ice is… well, cold would be an apt descriptor, but what if I didn't mean *that* ice? Sometimes ice is a verb, like when you ice a cake. Sometimes ice is a noun, as in when it is frozen water or an illegal substance. Sometimes, it can be used quite brutally to ice someone, which is a verb again. It can be a proper noun – think Vanilla Ice or Ice-T. On other occasions it can form a noun group in the form of an adjective – "It was ice cold". It really does depend on the context; there is no singular definition or answer that acts as a global definition for the word.

Is this the case with inquiry? Not in the sense that it can be a certain word classification, but moreover, is it possible to posit some dialectical thought around whether it is a subject or a pedagogy? I recognise that in the previous sentence I may have triggered some people's blood pressure to rise and possibly even scoff or hurl the book through an open window.

For those who maintained a firm grip on the book – thanks, and welcome to the next few sentences. Feel free to fill your colleagues in later.

This chapter explores the following content:
- Making a case for a pedagogy vs making a case for a subject
- Are we ever really in one stage on an inquiry?
- How do planners work?
- A piece of the action
- Come together
- Books and walls (and messages sent unwittingly)
- But why inquiry?

In so many curricula around the world, the word subject is not evident. Schools seem to take curriculum (which is divided neatly into 'learning areas') and in turn, turn them into stand-alone subjects or they integrate them under broader umbrella subjects. Schools do this with inquiry, it is no different. I grew up in a school that did Studies of Society and Environment (SOSE). That covered all sorts of learning such as History, Geography, Civics or what we may now call 'The Humanities'. When did we do it? Well, after lunch a few times a week. Was it inquiry? Certainly not. We were taught information, questioned on what we were taught and dutifully reproduced the learning we had in poster form at the end of the term on an A2 poster page. Subsequently, this was marked out of 10, a coloured star stuck on, brief comment added, before my parents rolled it up and placed an elastic band around it for safe storage.

But does this sound anything like inquiry these days in some schools?

Long has the debate passed that inquiry is a subject. It is a pedagogical approach, a way of learning that is natural and can be applied to any area of learning both inside and outside schools. But if inquiry isn't a subject, why do we have to explicitly teach the process? Perhaps, after all, it actually has content and needs to be taught – therefore, potentially making it a subject.

Making a case for a pedagogy vs making a case for a subject

Pedagogy: Kuhlthau, Maniotes and Caspari (2007) make the case nicely that inquiry is pedagogical as it is an approach which is a social process and has a high reliance on social interaction. Coupling this with students actively constructing their own knowledge makes the case for this constructivist approach to be just that: an approach.

Subject: Do our students need to actually learn how to inquire? Hopefully not is the answer, but if we are going to introduce a process or set of language around inquiry, then there needs to be some explicit teaching there. Whether it is consistency of terminology or displays or some other form, it is imperative that our students know the process – in some sense, they are learning the inquiry process.

I'm intentionally being provocative by suggesting it could be a subject, with the hope that you've had a response of sorts that has at least made you spark some thoughts of your own.

> *"Inquiry is not about getting to the right answer. Inquiry is about staying open to possibility, being comfortable with uncertainty, being prepared to arrive at an unexpected destination"*
> – **Kath Murdoch (2021)**

Are we ever really in one stage on an inquiry?

Whether you use Kath Murdoch's model (2015), 5Es (Bybee, 1997), Scientific Inquiry (Pedaste et al, 2015) or any other of the numerous incarnations, it is quite challenging to believe that at any given time students are all at the same stage at the same time.

We have no notion of what is happening inside their heads. We may have planned for a session where we are introducing the students to some initial experiences we have planned for a particular stage. Most likely it will be expressed as one of the following: Tuning in, Immersion, Engaging or Provocation. Regardless of the label we ascribe to it, we cannot determine the thinking that is occurring inside the students' minds. They may well be making connections, reflecting, enacting, explaining to themselves, drawing conclusions, feeling tension and other possibilities.

We are like a DJ at a booth in a nightclub. Being a DJ is like being a teacher of inquiry-based learning in that they both require a great deal of creativity and a passion for the craft. There are sights and sounds happening all around us. Hopefully everyone is in the groove and vibing on what we are doing. A DJ must be able to take different songs and combine them in a way that is both creative and engaging. Similarly, a teacher of inquiry-based learning must be able to take different ideas and concepts and combine them in a way that is both imaginative and stimulating.

As a DJ you are in control of the music, but not the vibe or the flow. You can impact these through your actions and choices. Both DJs and teachers of inquiry-based learning must also be able to think on their feet and improvise when needed. A great teacher gets a sense of where the learning needs to go next and respond accordingly.

Both DJs and teachers of inquiry-based learning must also have a strong understanding of their craft in order to be successful. Not just a knowledge, but an understanding. It cannot be surface or shallow. A DJ must have a deep understanding of different genres of music and the many techniques of mixing and blending. Similarly, a teacher of inquiry-based learning must have a deep understanding of different nuances of learning, the mood of their students, their prior knowledge, experiences or passions. Ultimately, both DJs and teachers of inquiry-based learning must also be able to think critically and respond in an instant to the mood/vibe of those around them.

Mid-performance, we expect DJs to adjust, crank up the bass and overlay a new track, fading up and fading through. They are, in reality, playing the role of an inquiry-based teacher: they are skilful, adept and responsive, feeding off the atmosphere and the needs of the room. What are the levers we need to pull when in a classroom? Do we have a back catalogue of hits and obscure references to make it all work? Do we read the room, feel it and go there?

No one goes to a nightclub to have a rest, they go for the atmosphere, the feel of the moments shared and the experiences had. They are willing participants on a journey with the DJ who they know knows how to guide them. I wonder how many of our students get out of bed in the morning hoping for the same, but knowing their reality will not be anything like this.

It is hard to determine who is in control of the learning and when. There will be times where the teacher takes the lead, others when there is a balance, and others where the teacher is acting as a facilitator and the students take control. In between is every possible nuanced variation. But this isn't meta-analysis of an entire inquiry (although true); it can be at a lesson level. Skilled inquiry teachers navigate and change gears between all these roles in a single session. There is a sense of ease when you witness an expert in inquiry learning going about their business – this mastery comes with hard work, learning, errors and practice.

Getting your driver's licence is a considerable achievement. When you are learning to drive, everything is manual and isolated. You drive, do a head check, change gear, indicate, turn the wheel and change lanes. There is a sense of routine and steps to this. If someone asked you to turn up the radio, that may just be too much to handle, as it is something else that is new and different. After driving for a while there is a sense of automaticity, to the degree where quite often drivers reflect and say, "I don't even remember driving for part of the way". While we don't want this level of mental absence, the fact they were doing all those things without even realising is the essence of what a practiced inquiry-learning teacher looks like in action.

So, how do we document such a seemingly chaotic and abstract process?

How do planners work?

The inquiry process is cyclical/hierarchical, but planners juxtapose the reality of what it looks like in a classroom setting – messy!

Typically, this is how planners are completed: left to right or top to bottom is the soup du jour. Pretty simply, we articulate the learning experiences chronologically in a document that works its way down a page like a list. Or we do it from left to right.

Top to bottom using Kathy Short's model (2009):

Inquiry Stage	Learning Experiences
Connection	
Invitation	
Tension	
Investigation	
Demonstration	
Revision	
Representation	
Valuation	
Action	

Left to right:

Inquiry Stage	Connection	Invitation	Tension	Investigation	Demonstration	Revision	Representation	Valuation	Action
Learning Experiences									

Both of these models suggest a linear approach to working and that the cycle is not circular or dynamic, rather it is worked through systematically. Short never designed her model to look like this or never to be used like this. Her actual inquiry process has arrows indicating a dynamism, responsiveness and flow of learning that reflects the learning naturally rather than literally in order.

Similarly, Kath Murdoch (2015), although a more digestible five-step process, still didn't design the inquiry process to be adhered to from a 'start to finish' approach. Her model has arrows that show the ebb and flow of learning and the dynamic nature of an inquiry.

Yet, in both instances, in good faith, many teachers have dedicated their time to creating planners that do exactly the opposite of what the inquiry process they are following stands for. A wise principal of mine once said, "Don't come to me with problems, come to me with solutions." So, I have presented a problem and now a little voice in my head tells me to present a solution – thanks, Des!

Here is a possible solution to design a planner that covers all the dynamism of an actual inquiry while allowing teachers to document it in a chronological manner.

This time using Murdoch's model:

	Designing Engaging Learning Experiences			
Inquiry Process	Tune In	Find Out/Sort Out	Go Further	Reflect and Act
Inquiry Stage Description	*Establish purpose and relevance; Provoke curiosity and wonder; Access and document prior knowledge, existing theories and ideas; Formulate questions; Consider ways to find out*	*Use a range of resources and methods to gather information (read, view, interview, survey, experiment, observe…); Aim to connect with people, places and objects to broaden understanding; Critically assess the value of the information gathered; Document information gathered in a range of ways; Make sense of the information gathered; Analyse, organise, compare, contrast, sift and sort; Reflect, respond and express new thinking; Revisit questions, refine and add new ones*	*Use new questions as the basis for extended inquiry; Establish personal pathways of interest; Share new learnings with others*	*Generalise, predict, reflect, evaluate, hypothesise, create, prove, plan, justify, suggest, argue, compose, prioritise, design, construct, perform, invent, conclude, criticise, debate, explain, give reasons, grade, judge, recommend, support, test, validate*

Inquiry is messy – but what is it? **11**

At face value, this looks exactly like a traditional planner that doesn't reflect anything like the promised solution. But what if the planner was filled out row by row rather than column by column? Well then, that would mean there would be lots of rows at the bottom of the table. Yes, there would be. But let's have each one of them represent the sequence of learning and the learning experience will be documented under the intended stage of the inquiry.

Now we have a planner that shows the reflexive nature of an inquiry process and inquiry as well as showing the sequence the learning has taken…

Designing Engaging Learning Experiences

Inquiry Process	Tune In	Find Out/Sort Out	Go Further	Reflect and Act
Inquiry Stage Description	*Establish purpose and relevance; Provoke curiosity and wonder; Access and document prior knowledge, existing theories and ideas; Formulate questions; Consider ways to find out*	*Use a range of resources and methods to gather information (read, view, interview, survey, experiment, observe...); Aim to connect with people, places and objects to broaden understanding; Critically assess the value of the information gathered; Document information gathered in a range of ways; Make sense of the information gathered; Analyse, organise, compare, contrast, sift and sort; Reflect, respond and express new thinking; Revisit questions, refine and add new ones*	*Use new questions as the basis for extended inquiry; Establish personal pathways of interest; Share new learnings with others*	*Generalise, predict, reflect, evaluate, hypothesise, create, prove, plan, justify, suggest, argue, compose, prioritise, design, construct, perform, invent, conclude, criticise, debate, explain, give reasons, grade, judge, recommend, support, test, validate*
	Activity 1	*Activity 2*	*Activity 3*	
	Activity 4			
	Activity 5			
	Activity 6	*Activity 7*		

A piece of the action

How dare you want to take action – we are not up to that section yet! Are you guilty of saying that? I sincerely hope not. And if you are, please read on, as there is a solution in sight. If you are not guilty of saying that, has your adherence to following an inquiry process indirectly communicated that to your student? I'll give you an example…

In many classrooms around the world there are inquiries that have a sustainability lens – amazing (if only every classroom around the world did this!). In the initial experiences offered to students, you may look at different ways to save energy or even explore where energy comes from; we may mess around with circuits, batteries and alligator clips. We would document that quite safely in our 'tuning in' section if we used Murdoch's model. If then, the next day, a student comes into class and says, "I went home last night and told my parents we have to save energy and be more sustainable. I told them I would turn out the light after leaving a room!", what is your response?

- Do you honour the action?
- Do you ignore it, as it would really mess up the planning you had done for three weeks' time?
- Do you thank them and quietly move on?
- Do you celebrate it and get the whole class to listen?
- Do you celebrate it by getting them to record it on an action wall?
- Are they front and centre at assembly next week to be celebrated by the community?

I have certainly been guilty of not celebrating student action earlier in my career. So, if we don't celebrate it, what message are we sending? In essence, the message is, "That is good that you did that at home, now where was I up to in our inquiry?"

It is quite possible to have completely disempowered an engaged learner – that is about as cardinal a sin in learning as I can imagine. It sits alongside ignoring student voice – as in so many ways it literally and metaphorically is.

Come together

Whatever inquiry looks like in your school, there needs to be a singular understanding from all teachers – and I mean all: principals, heads of departments, single subject or specialist teachers, classroom teachers and everyone in between.

How do you go about ensuring that everyone is on the same page? Simply, you work together. Whether it is closure day, a guest speaker, a series of professional learning opportunities or another method, you need to approach this as a team. One organiser that I've used on many occasions is a Frayer model. The simplicity of the Frayer model is that it only has four components and each is very accessible. But having a Frayer model and using it well are different beasts altogether.

People need to use evidence, facts, knowledge and research to fill one out in this instance. You can just fill it out with your own perception and then have everyone share theirs and operate in the hope that you come to a consensus. That may work, but does it allow for each member of staff to develop a different understanding?

With some carefully selected material (guest speaker, clip, reading, etc) you can introduce the whole staff to inquiry. One of my favourites is Lydia, the Fairy Scientist (www.youtube.com/watch?v=akk5EvTMGKo). This is heavily weighted toward a scientific inquiry and if this is not the version of inquiry you wish for your school community, then you have two choices:

1. Include it in the session and lead staff toward this being the non-example – this could only occur if you had some actual examples first, however.
2. Leave it out entirely.

Choose your stimulus carefully and model the behaviour you wish to develop. Provide staff with some stimuli and leave it open for them to do some personal inquiry also. I am so pleased to see a recent change in presenter approach where presenters/speakers are now aligning their mode of delivery to match their pedagogical position. Nothing screams hypocrisy like a session on inquiry learning that is all just a talkfest from the presenter!

Allowing time and space for your staff to be learners and feel the graft is key.

Books and walls (and messages sent unwittingly)

When you review your student book list, what is the rationale behind the books? Traditionally, it is something like this:

- 12 lined books (6 for Literacy, 2 for homework, 1 for SEL/RE, 2 for specialists, 1 spare just in case
- 2 grid books for Maths
- 2 scrapbooks/project books for inquiry

The order is placed, they are delivered to school via a company or brought from home and we ask students to label them. Call this one 'reading', this one 'writing', this one 'inquiry', this one 'maths', etc. But then we claim to integrate or offer inquiry.

Sixteen books in total, whether that is accurate or not, is not the point I'm illustrating. The point is we are, through the selection and labelling of books, informing our students that these are distinct subjects that bear no relationship with any others and never shall we do anything that resembles a blurring of lines. Then we have the audacity to say we are integrating or covering some of the inquiry through my Literacy block.

If we are covering inquiry through Literacy, then my question would be, "Which skills or content are being addressed?" If you are using Literacy skills to engage in inquiry content, then does it matter what you call the subject? Does it need a label? Isn't it just learning, after all?

Could the same argument be had for classroom walls? Absolutely it could. I always prided myself on being terrible at wall displays; I would outsource this at any given chance to peers or my wife – as it was not my strength. I could never get the bunting straight to divide my writing wall from my inquiry wall. Until one day, years later, I asked myself: 'why do I have to have walls dedicated to certain types of learning?' It turned out, I didn't!

But that led me to the wondering… 'How do I display the learning across the room?' An epiphanic moment had occurred. Suddenly, I could see that all learning was indeed learning and that there were skills and content that needed to be shared with students, but not bound by arbitrary titles or spaces. We know that learners with English as an additional language (EAL) may well have a strength in Mathematics, but without the Literacy skills behind it, they struggle to demonstrate their learning. Arbitrary subject names impede learning, students learn in silos and have little to no conceptual development or connection between learning areas.

The learning space (and the books) became bound by the inquiry, not by subjects. We would engage in a new inquiry, so that meant that we needed a new book – a book that held all our learning in it – Literacy, Maths and inquiry. If we truly link our Reading, Writing and Maths to inquiry, why would we separate them out into different books? Similarly, the walls in the classroom became centred on our inquiry. The key learning was central in the display space and links were made.

One way of demonstrating this is by covering the walls with butcher's paper (or other such paper) and essentially having a blank canvas. And if inquiry learning is an art form, that is quite an appropriate starting point. The displays are built and developed over time with the students. This is a world away from the 'Pinterest-styled classrooms' that dominate social media feeds and are aspired to by so many.

But why inquiry?

If you have ever had the experience of looking at a property, either for rental or for purchase, you get the option to send an email enquiry to the agent. Why they chose enquiry or inquiry I'm not sure, but the words are interchangeable and both mean the same thing. So, when you enquire (or inquire) about a property, you are in essence engaging in the process of asking questions, or trying to find information about a topic.

Isn't that exactly what we want our students or learners to be doing? Of course, it is a resounding "yes". These things don't happen by chance – they are something intentional and planned that a school has to set for its pedagogical approach. Teachers need professional development in the area, and scaffolds and consistency of language need to exist robustly.

As a parent of three, I have seen them experience quite a range of educators within the one school setting. Yet, the pedagogy was expressed as the same. Factors like experience, comfort levels, skill sets, dispositions, etc, are all real. The challenge for schools is to ensure there is consistency across the school and in all classrooms. No student should win or lose the teacher lottery by getting the 'good one' or the 'one no one wants'. That kind of thinking isn't helpful, nor is it necessary for the conditions to exist. Guaranteeing low levels of variability between teachers is essential to ensure the levels of consistency with the pedagogical approach is achieved.

Inquiry can look different in different settings, and indeed it should. But across a school setting there should be low levels of variability in what it looks like and how it functions. As a school you need to decide on some non-negotiables, such as:

- What 'version' of inquiry you will adopt
- What process you will follow
- What planners will look like
- What classroom displays should include

- What resourcing for students is required
- What teacher/student participation levels should look like and how they vary

Chapter summary

- Establish what inquiry means in your setting.
- Develop a planner that reflects the pedagogy – and get creative!
- Include as many staff as possible in conversations and decision-making about pedagogy.
- There are different models of inquiry – whichever you choose, honour it and be consistent across the school.
- Consider how your booklists reflect your pedagogy.
- Consider what role displays play in supporting or provoking the learning.
- Desire a community of learners where inquiry is the pedagogical position.
- Schools need to work hard to have a singular pedagogical position and try to ensure low levels of variability across their teaching staff.

Reflection

Ask yourself or your team these questions and journal the responses. Keep them aside and then after a period of time (a term at least) come back to them and see how your thinking has progressed.

- Could you have one book per inquiry? Just one per inquiry and all goes in there.
- Could your students begin to see the connection and stop asking the question: "Are we doing reading or writing or inquiry?"
- Could they adapt to a new paradigm? One where new norms are developed and lines don't just get blurred, they aren't even present.
- Could your walls and classroom displays reinforce this notion of learning being connected and not be bound by subject?
- Could your language reinforce this by not mentioning subject, but refer to skills?

CHAPTER 2

CONCEPTUAL FRAMEWORK

"He who fails to plan is planning to fail"
– **Winston Churchill (attributed)**

*"We get some rules to follow. That and this, these and those.
No one knows"*
– **Queens of the Stone Age: 'No One Knows'**

It is deep into November, almost December, and in the southern hemisphere that means a few things for teachers:

1. Report writing (possibly with the added bonus of learning conversations with parents/students)
2. All learning needs to be tied up and finalised for the school year
3. And the upcoming onslaught of glitter in primary classrooms

But the learning finishes.

We know that it will continue for those who are still attending school the next year, but the notion is that schools stop. It is not unique that the institution closes, there is cricket season, netball season, etc. But many industries continue after a few key dates off. Hospitals don't stop as a result of the date on a calendar.

Please don't misinterpret this as advocating for schools being open longer or not being in need of a well-deserved respite from school life. It is merely a commentary that we have a finite period each year, be it calendar or school, we stop.

However, it is not just at the end of the school year that we stop. We do it on three (or another number, depending on the location) other occasions over the course of the year. These holidays punctuate the school year and learning has to be completed before they come or else. This chapter will explore the 'else', the 'else' being: What would/could happen if instead of finishing learning during the school year schools flipped the model – could they attempt to accommodate learning first and holidays second? Can schools press pause instead of stop?

Most schools are, as expressed above, lock-stepped into delivering learning that is bound by time. Learning is a far more organic process and the curriculum is crowded. This chapter will explore the different ways in which learning can be allocated conceptually. Using macro-concepts that are universal in nature and are not bound to domain/silo-style learning, this chapter will explore how to create broader and more significant areas to inquire into – rather than the term or semester boundaries.

This chapter will explore why we do what we do and challenge some preconceived notions through the following sections:

- **Pause for thought**
- **Lessons from Uno**
- **What sort of process can be used?**
- **Are these concepts or their definitions set in stone?**

Pause for thought

Have you ever paused to consider that in most North American, European and English-speaking countries learning stops on the Thursday before the first Sunday after the full moon that occurs on or after the spring equinox in the northern hemisphere or the autumnal equinox in the southern hemisphere?

Complicated? We call it Easter.

If someone was to instruct you to stop your learning on the Tuesday after Gemini was in the Taurean sky (I have no idea if this is possible), I would hope you would rightly question their logic. It seems arbitrary and potentially capricious. Learning surely must come first, rather than an astrological or astronomic event. Yet, every Easter, we stop the learning and consign our inquiry to the completed pile.

If you've been teaching for a few years, it is highly likely you've experienced the following two scenarios. I hope it is more often the second one that resonates with you, rather than the first.

It is Term 3, Week 6. The students groan when they see your outline for the day and there is an 'inquiry' lesson listed. You have four more weeks to go – maybe five if it is a particularly cruel term. You've stretched the learning to get this far. You have realised that there is nothing left in this inquiry to teach, as the students have not connected with it, and the students have literally run out of passion or drive for your inquiry. Yet there are still four weeks to go. So many lessons to pad and fill. So many blank sections of a work program staring loom large, daring you to fill them with something meaningful. But you can't. But you have to. So, you do, only it isn't powerful learning, it is filler.

Conversely, it is Term 3, Week 10. The students cheer when they see your outline for the day and there is an 'inquiry' lesson listed. You only have a few days to go until the holidays and the inquiry is NOWHERE near completed. Time has flown by. The students are engaged. You are engaged. But it doesn't matter, as in a few days' time, the inquiry is over, the holidays will begin and the learning will stop. Such rich learning opportunities potentially await, but will never be realised due to the holidays. So, you truncate the learning, tying it up with activities that, instead of enhancing learning, assess and finalise it. The students don't want to stop and you have that blissful learning hum. So few blank sections of a work program staring loom large, daring you to fill them with something meaningful. But you can't. But you have to. So, you do, only it isn't powerful learning, it is shutting learning down.

Lessons from Uno

Here is a leadership team: Jason, Sally, Troy and Jess. They divide into two groups: Jason and Sally, and Troy and Jess. These two teams are about to play a few games of Uno.

Jason and Sally play a quick game with decisiveness and some nasty 'Draw 4s' from Jason. He's on Uno in no time and has the same colour as the last card played. Sally sweats with 15 cards and she is about to pick up, hoping for something, anything. At the same time, Troy and Jess are on a consistent run of playing a few cards, picking up and a bit of friendly skipping. Both of them have five cards left and neither is supremely confident yet. Upon hearing Jason's Uno call and look at Sally's hand, they smile, grateful for their relative position.

Jason plays his last card and sits back, replete with his handy work, while Sally shuffles the deck in the hope of redemption. Their second game begins while Troy and Jess are shuffling as well – only not to finish their game, they are shuffling the played cards to continue their first game.

Jason, with the luck of the draw on his side, knows that what he has been dealt in the second hand will just about guarantee him another win. He is planning out his moves four or five in advance. Sally, meanwhile, laments her collection of cards. It is over pretty swiftly. Not long after Jason's second win, in the other game Jess emerges victorious against Troy.

Both teams played for around the same amount of time. One team squeezed in two games, while the other completed a longer one. Both run their natural course and were as long as they needed to be. While the length couldn't be predetermined, neither was stopped by an external force. If it was predetermined that both teams had to play Uno for a set period of time, what would Jason and Sally have done after they had finished? This is what happens when we plan learning for an arbitrary period of time that is bound by holidays.

While this appears to advocate against planning learning to be set in time periods, it is more nuanced than that. The above is a consideration to hold that learning shouldn't be bound by the school term. With careful curation, consideration and planning, you can almost anticipate the length you dedicate toward the learning. This is when you use your context, knowledge of the students, the content and reporting accountabilities, and interest of the students to make decisions about learning.

When planning learning, this is what we do. It is what we do naturally.

So, how can you design inquiries to map across the year?

What sort of process can be used?

There are no shortcuts to be had here. Having a leadership team or leader singularly design these is not only disempowering, but it also deprives the staff of the opportunities to learn and work together. There has to be an intentional, active and collaborative process as a staff. The following are offered as a three-step process:

- **Identifying** the macro concepts
- **Refining** the macro concepts
- **Defining** on the macro concepts

Identifying the macro concepts

Butcher's paper, markers, Post-it notes along with a shared cognitive load are all the tools you need. Your school may wish to use a digital platform.

This is highly contextualised and needs to reflect the learning and learners of your school. Engage in a process that removes curriculum from the equation – the last thing you need here is teachers thinking the big concepts are Maths, English, Science, etc.

Provide time, space and provocations to allow staff to engage in conversations about what broad concepts learning can be organised into. There is no right or wrong answer, only what works best for your school context.

The strategy of Chalk Talk (Ritchhart's Thinking Routine, 2011) is a great way to engage learning and removing the dominant voice. The process is simple and extremely quiet as talking is banned. The conversations all take place on paper.

- Have statements, words or images (any stimulus) written in the middle of a large piece of paper.
- Staff are to respond to the stimulus by either writing a question or directly commenting on it.
- As staff rotate through the different papers, they can answer or ask a question or provide a comment. Should they agree or disagree, that can be done, too! All responses are valid.
- Staff need to have visited each paper and then return to re-view their starting point to see the conversation that took place.

Some suggestions for the questions on the papers would be:

- What is worth learning about?
- Without mentioning a subject, what do our students need to learn more about?
- What do you wish you had more time to teach your students about?
- What do you wish you learnt more about at school?
- What have the best inquiries you've 'taught' been about?
- What concepts are worth exploring?
- Is sustainability taught?
- I don't need to teach conflict management as it isn't in the curriculum.
- History is taught by the History teacher.
- When is the concept of time taught?

Review each stimulus and see if themes emerge. If they don't, staff will need to group the statements recorded into broad themes. If the word **change** comes up often, then that may well be a macro concept. Imagine if you ended up with 37 macro concepts – they would be very short inquiries! But if you do have 37, seek a broader umbrella concept that covers them. It may be that you can't decide between **identity** or **humanity**. Could you merge those two and call one macro concept *Identity and Humanity*?

If this is a predetermined notion of how many would work for your school, this needs to be shared early as it may support staff in making final decisions. When staff are refining their thinking, it may help to have some parameters in which to work.

Another possibility is that the leadership team analyse the Chalk Talk responses from the staff and aggregate them on behalf of the staff and then present them back. It can be quite challenging to get absolute consensus from a large group, and they may well thank leadership for doing some of the heavy lifting to then present back a synthesised version of their input. Presenting them back to the staff for review and feedback/revision is as important as seeking their initial input.

Identifying the macro concepts is the first step in the process of developing a conceptual framework, next comes their refining in order to define them.

Refining the macro concepts

Arriving at a list of macro concepts that the staff have collaborated to create sets the scene, but it doesn't provide the necessary scope or definition for all to understand. At this stage there are singular words or concepts allocated and yet to be fully articulated – and they need refining.

They need to be refined as interpretation and individual perception need to be removed in the interest of consistency of understanding. In this sense, we are seeking consistency and low levels of variability in the staff's understanding of what each of these concepts actually means.

How easy would it be to just do this on behalf of the staff? But how disempowering! It would be easier to give the staff the answers or look the macro concepts up in a dictionary or use the internet to search the macro concepts or seek an 'expert's' input but… you get out what you put in… And, as such, this requires time and collaboration.

Depending on your context, the question(s) that need to be asked include:
- What do they mean to you as a staff?

- What do they mean to your students?
- What do they mean to your parents?
- What do they mean to your community?
- What do they mean to your school?

The following is offered as a process to follow with the staff to gain their consistent understanding of the macro concepts.

At a staff meeting, staff are mixed into groups that are representative of the diverse roles and places in the school staff operate in.

Pose the question: If you could describe the areas of learning that would take place with *(insert your first macro concept here)* – what would they be? Staff, using large pieces of paper and markers, record in their groups what their thoughts are.

Next, the staff need to know that after the first macro concept, they will share back. This will help them understand how others have interpreted the task but may also act to confirm that their thinking was on the right path. It may even trigger further thinking and recording. But the opportunity to hear other viewpoints is rich in its dissonance. It can also act as an opportunity to validate thinking. There may well be a staff member who was a lone voice in their group, but through listening to other groups realises that every other group came up with the same (formerly) obscure offering.

Setting a time limit for each macro concept may support the progress of groups.

Here is an example of what one may look like...

These inquiries will focus on:

- How people treat each other
- Aspects of health
- Different cultures and cultural histories

Reviewing after the first completed one provides the opportunity for groups to then take time to reflect on their contributions. Staff get to review what they have recorded and see if the same word appears on more than one page. Then, if they have this happenstance, make a decision as to whether it needs to be omitted from one or more of the areas or leave things as they are. Remember, at this stage (as with many), there are no right or wrong answers.

It also provides a different opportunity for ideas to be planted. Through observations, if it is noticed an element that is deemed as important is absented through the groups' thinking, then the question needing to be asked is, "If you had to put the word _____ on to one of your pages, where would you put it?" If there are certain elements that have been discussed in alternate forums that there is a desire to see in here, float those also. Be careful to challenge thinking, not direct it. Directing thinking in this instance is disempowering and provides the space for staff to become more passive with the thought that you have a preconceived notion of what the school wants from this process. And it does – it is to work through the process collaboratively!

The next step is to collect and collate all the responses. Type up the responses (or if it was recorded digitally, copy and paste them all onto one document) for each of the macro concepts. Next, paste these into a word cloud generator. The following image is a word cloud reflecting input of six groups for one macro concept:

Word clouds are such a precious time-saving (and aesthetic) way of presenting the main themes or ideas generated. Present them and share them with the staff, in order for them to re-engage in the thinking required. How powerful to know how your colleagues thought. With these created for each of your macro concepts, you are on well on the journey to refining the thinking to achieve consensus.

Defining on the macro concepts

Whether this process takes place with the whole staff, the leadership team or assigned groups, there needs to be a consistency in their construction.

Using the word clouds to provide stimulus and reorientation into the thinking, provide the parameters of what you want the definitions to read like.

It may also help to provide an example to illustrate what it could look like. If dot points are sought, ask for them; in my experience, they are preferable as it sharpens thinking, and sentence construction/prose can hinder the thought process.

> We need to create four or five dot points to define this macro concept. Let's begin with the sentence starter:
>
> The learning in *(insert macro concept)* focuses on…
>
> - (Dot points recorded here)
> -
> -

Define the thinking as much as possible. Agree, disagree, engage in cognitive conflict, but establish definitions that are accessible for all staff and that are accessible for any staff that join the team in coming years. Try to avoid jargon or terms that are specific to your setting. However, if there are terms that are specific to your setting, ensure that all new staff can be inducted into their meaning and that they are comfortable in applying these in your setting.

At this stage, the staff may need to 'sit' with them. Provide the staff with a window in which feedback is invited. Share the macro concept working definitions digitally or print off individual copies, so staff members have access to them. Print them off and display them in public or communal areas where staff gather. Grab a wad of Blu-Tak and stick it to the wall near the posters with a marker stuck in it. Encourage the staff to write on them. Questions and comments are equally valid. Ideally, it promotes opportunities for the staff to continue to engage in the thinking in this space.

But if you are going to invite feedback, then you need to respond to it. After a period of time, take the posters down and honour the thinking of your colleagues. That doesn't mean change just because. It means in some forum, staff meeting, working party, pedagogical leadership team or other, review the feedback. Any feedback that enhances the working definitions should be included. With any feedback that is semantic in nature, be discerning and discuss (and ultimately decide on) which language best suits your context. Then, finally, part with the feedback that isn't generative or does not enhance the definitions.

Are these concepts or their definitions set in stone?

As with any practice, review enhances understanding or has the potential to enhance the existing. Engage in a cycle of review even when things are going well. After all, reflective practice and growth are symbiotic in their relationship. When new staff come on board, they bring their perception and experiences, which may add to the existing understanding. Over time, our own experiences impact and refine our own perceptions.

There are many practices and structures in school that are static when they could or should be dynamic. So, be dynamic.

If, as a result of the review process, there are fundamental changes, these changes are profound in nature and need to be respected and responded to. This may well lead to a complete remapping of the curriculum. In which case, ensure you have the processes and time required for the scope of work intended.

There may well be questions circling around your mind, such as:

- Can an inquiry bridge a term?
- How do you report on learning if it bridges a term?
- Do the macro concepts have to align across the school?
- Can units start and finish over the course of the year at different times in different levels?

These are addressed in Chapter 7, along with how a year can be planned out and developed to ensure breadth and depth across.

Chapter summary

- Reflect and decide on how long your inquiries will last – will they bridge terms or other artificial structures?
- Learning is organic, yet the structures we have are quite static. Learning doesn't need to be confined to these structures – it is possible to 'ignore them' in the name of learning.

- Collaboratively develop a process of identifying the conceptual framework in which to map curriculum against.
- Be as inclusive as possible at all stages of the conceptual development.
- Sit with the work done and reflect before finalising.
- Invite reflections, feedback and contributions from all staff.
- Be prepared to map curriculum against these concepts.

Reflection: How long does it take to play a game of Uno? That is the reflection activity for this chapter. Readers are led through a potential staff activity that involves all staff playing multiple games of Uno – knowing that some are longer and some are shorter – and that is perfect!

Reflection

Go out and purchase enough packs of Uno to play with the staff (or just two to be used with a team – so long as there are at least two games going on).

This is the fun part – play a few games.

- **Stop all games at an arbitrary timeframe.** Ask the players how they felt with the game stopped.
- **When do they finish?** All together? What do you notice about the finishing times of each game? Was it exactly the same?
- **Draw the parallels out.** Ask how this relates to the learning and inquiries when we plan and teach them.

Or:

- **Tell everyone that their game has to last exactly three minutes and 24 seconds.** How close do they get to the time? Ask how they feel or felt during that.
- **Draw the parallels out.** Ask how this relates to the learning and inquiries when we plan and teach them.

Whichever direction…

- **After you've finished the session.** Check if anyone actually goes back to finish their game. What does that say about a task/learning when we stop it?

CHAPTER 3

MAPPING CURRICULUM

*"A curriculum map is exactly that – a map.
And maps should inspire possibilities rather than limit options"*
– **John Spencer (2017)**

*"Where are you going my beautiful friend?
Is this the road that you take till the end?"*
– **Big Audio Dynamite: 'The Globe'**

Curriculum mapping is far from unchartered territory, in fact, it is territory we all know and follow (with varying degrees of fidelity depending on the setting). We've heard the term and it can be applied in many different ways. For the purpose of this book, the following is the incarnation curriculum mapping takes.

Curriculum mapping is the articulation and expression of a written curriculum plotted against predetermined concepts and/or allocated periods of time. The process outlined in this chapter will provide teachers with an approach that is flexible enough to be mapped against any curricula while providing flexibility for localised timeframes and contexts.

*"Curriculum mapping, showing the relationships of all aspects
of the curriculum, is a linchpin to attain the objectives/outcomes
of any curriculum. It illustrates the relationship between
the different components of the curriculum so that all the
connections are easily visualized"*
– **Harden RM (2001)**

Pilots don't get to decide where they fly – it is on their roster, their predetermined route. They experience little agency and autonomy in the destination. They are highly trained and highly skilled, they are adept at taking off, adjusting being in control of an inordinate number of buttons, lights, levers, switches, etc. They can adjust mid-flight and the passengers have little to no knowledge of the countless decisions being made on their behalf to keep them safe and on target. But the destination is never in doubt, not for the passengers nor the flight crew.

Imagine walking through the airport about to board your flight to Fiji, with visions of yourself poolside, the sun warming you and the cares and stresses of your day-to-day life melting away like the ice cubes in your drink. Imagine the pilot walking through the same terminal building thinking to herself, 'I wonder where I am going today?'.

Worse still would be the pilot knowing where she is going and then deciding, 'I don't feel much like Singapore today, Winnipeg it is for me!' Nothing against Singapore, but if you've been there last year and were eager for a new destination, with new experiences and were not expecting to go there again, well, there would be a level of disappointed. Not only that, but you would be ill-equipped in your suitcase. Those Okanui board shorts aren't going to keep out the bracing winds coming off the Manitoban prairies!

In a similar way, we have to know where we are going before we 'take off' for a new school year. After a school has determined how it will divide the curriculum up, be it terms (why would you stick to terms when you don't have to?), three themes, six macro concepts, eight throughlines, then comes the task of curriculum allocation across these. There is no right or wrong, just the framework or incarnation that works in your particular context. A further consideration is that of who will be experiencing the learning. This will be determined again by local context and curriculum accountabilities.

The importance of curriculum mapping cannot be understated, as it sets the foundation for great teaching, if done well. The Grattan Institute (2022) produced a paper *Ending the lesson lottery: How to improve curriculum planning in schools*. The findings are articulated as such: "A whole-school curriculum map, which is a coordinated plan for how a school will implement its curriculum. This plan is often organised by subject area and details every unit being taught, including what content and skills will be covered, and how and when they will be assessed. This plan provides school leaders with a bird's-eye view of their school's curriculum."

This chapter will explore how this can be done using six macro concepts over a two-year scope and sequence using the Victorian Curriculum standards.

The process itself, once the manner in which the curriculum is going to be allocated is organised, is as follows:
- **Honouring student voice**
- **Building a template**
- **Sharing the template**
- **Setting the scene**
- **Mapping the curriculum**
- **Reviewing the mapping**

Honouring student voice

Student voice can come (or not appear at all) in schools at different points. Infusing it early in the planning process has potential benefits that should be considered.

> *"Student voice is most successful when it enables students to feel that they are members of a learning community, that they matter, and that they have something valuable to offer"*
> – **Ruddock (2007)**

Honouring student voice at this early stage demonstrates the importance of their inclusion and active participation in what is ultimately their learning. It also provides the important concept of listening and engaging with students to support our understanding of the learning they wish to undertake.

There are many ways in which to capture student thinking; simply having a conversation with focus groups, cohorts or the whole class. Alternatively, producing a sheet with questions like the following:

- What are you interested in learning about?
- What have you learnt before that has interested you?
- Think about a previous inquiry, what was it that made it memorable?
- What was your favourite thing to learn last year?
- What are your passions?
- What are your interests?
- What is the best way for you to learn? For example, hands on; with technology; discussions; research based; etc.
- If you could learn more about one thing, what would it be?

Imagine how easy this would be if when an inquiry 'finished', active feedback was sought from students. Keeping these on file, and ready to be brought out at the time of curriculum mapping, could prove to be an invaluable resource for supporting the development of upcoming inquiries.

Building a template

Creating a template that has all the content to be mapped curriculum is the first next step. This can be done in any meaningful way that suits the context and choice of the school. There is software available to support this process, however, a database of standards or outcomes needs to be input. The process is manual and a little time-consuming, but it is an investment in ensuring the steps afterwards are built on a solid foundation.

Using a spreadsheet, identify the subject areas/curriculum in a column. Colour code each column so that there is a consistency of Geography being purple in each tab of the spreadsheet. Then copy and paste curriculum standards/outcomes under the relevant heading. Following that same process over each tab (for each grade/level) of curriculum, you'll have something like the below...

Victorian Curriculum – Grades 1 and 2 – Colour coded and ready to be mapped

Intentionally omitted are Literacy and Mathematics from the curriculum mapping, as these can support the learning and communication skills during the individual inquiries. Likewise are specific content areas that would be covered by single-subject or specialist teachers such as The Arts, Languages, etc. These can be included, but for illustrative purposes have not been. In the next chapter, we will explore how to align Literacy and Mathematics to support the ongoing learning in inquiry (where applicable).

Sharing the template

A tale of two methodologies.

Digital or paper? Again, it has to be what will work best in your setting – local agency has to be a contributing factor. What works best in each school setting is not what works best for an individual person – but for the majority of those mapping the curriculum. The following (which are far from exhaustive) are for your consideration and are designed to help guide your decision:

Digital – the Good, the Bad and the Ugly		
The Good	The Bad	The Ugly
- Everything is shared with those who need access (provided it is online, for example, Google Docs, OneDrive, SharePoint, etc). - Changes are immediate and visible by all. - Version histories are retrievable (if online). - Saved centrally and accessible.	- Those with lower levels of tech savviness may struggle to engage. - Multiple screens may cause confusion.	- A couple of misplaced or ill-advised clicks can change a lot.

Paper – the Good, the Bad and the Ugly		
The Good	**The Bad**	**The Ugly**
• It is highly manipulable. • Lots of people can make changes simultaneously. • Focuses the group on one singular place. • Tactile experience.	• Pieces can go missing. • If you want to have something in both years, then it requires a second copy.	• Printing off copies. • At some point, someone will have to copy and paste to reflect this digitally.

Setting the scene

When mapping the curriculum, the consideration of where the students have been – not just where they are going – is a significant factor. Mapping curriculum without this is a recipe for potential mistakes. Conduct an audit on previous learning the students have engaged in over their time at the school. This will ensure there is breadth and/or depth to the learning experienced by the students. It is much harder to engage students in learning they have already done! In fact, you could argue there is no learning when there is repetition of content in this manner. It is as though the students are just watching a rerun with a different lead actor.

The two tables below demonstrate what the previous two years of learning are for the incoming Grade 3s:

Grade 2 2020			
Big Idea	Knowing ourselves and others helps build healthy relationships		
Inquiries into	How our learning community works	How my actions affect others	The characteristics of healthy relationships
Curriculum Covered	Health & Physical Education	Personal & Social Capabilities	
Big Idea	Where people live determines their lifestyle		
Inquiries into	Factors that determine where and how people live -resources available to them in that area	Types of structures around the world	Why structures in some places are made from different materials than others
Curriculum Covered	Geography	History	Ethical Capabilities
Big Idea	All children have rights and responsibilities		
Inquiries into	The responsibilities people have	The UN Declaration of the Rights of the Child	How children's responsibilities and access to rights differ
Curriculum Covered	Health & Physical Education		
Big Idea	Living things grow and change		
Inquiries into	Basic needs of living things	The way things grow and change	Caring for living things
Curriculum Covered	Science	Critical & Creative Thinking	Ethical Capabilities
Big Idea	Transport systems reflect the needs of the community		
Inquiries into	The features of a system	Transport systems are designed to meet the needs of the community	Transport connects and organises the community
Curriculum Covered	Personal & Social Capability	Ethical Capability	Critical & Creative Thinking

Grade 1 2019				
Big Idea	Being human is using kindness with ourselves and others			
Inquiries into	What is kindness	How our actions impact others	Being kind to myself and others	
Curriculum Covered	Personal & Social Capability	Ethical Capability	Health & Physical Education	
Big Idea	People's lives have changed over time			
Inquiries into	Personal and family histories	Experiences of life from the past to the present	The effect of changing technology on people's lives	
Curriculum Covered	History	Design & Technologies	Critical & Creative Thinking	
Big Idea	Messages without words can be a powerful form of communication			
Inquiries into	The many ways in which messages are communicated	The ways we individually respond to messages, shapes our point of view	How we decode, analyse and interpret to build our understanding	
Curriculum Covered	Design & Technologies	The Arts	Critical & Creative Thinking	
Big Idea	Weather and seasons impact on our daily lives			
Inquiries into	How seasons change throughout the year	The unique properties and features of seasons	Extreme weather and how it affects the environment	
Curriculum Covered	Geography	Science		
Big Idea	Communities function more effectively when there is a sense of responsibility			
Inquiries into	The purpose of rules, rights and responsibilities in our community	Individual and communal responsibility	Cause and effect in group situations	
Curriculum Covered	Geography	Critical & Creative Thinking	Ethical Capabilities	Personal & Social Capabilities
Big Idea	Plants are a life sustaining resource			
Inquiries into	The changes that occur through plant growth	Taking responsibility to care for plants as they grow	The role plants play in our lives	
Curriculum Covered	Science	Ethical Capability	Personal & Social Capabilities	

Next is the dilemma of who works with who. There are so many different ways this part can be conducted. Do we use this year's teams with their experience and knowledge of the curriculum to allocate? Do we use next year's teams as they are the ones going to be working in this space? Do we mix things up and have people from across the school in a different space? Working in the teams that will engage in this content in the coming year generates greater buy in and vested interest.

If we use next year's teams and there are outgoing staff, what should they do? There is so much experience and wisdom to be gained from people who have walked the path before. If they are available, then harness their knowledge. Occasionally, staff who are leaving are not in the mindset to be constructive in their final endeavours in a workplace – if this is the case, consider the impact they may have on the process.

Don't forget about leadership, specialist teachers and education support officers! They have a role to play – including them is a way of ensuring they feel connected to the classroom and the learning that occurs there. Leadership are teachers, too. They will have experience and insights that are well worth listening to. Many principals and deputy/assistant principals find themselves in roles that are further and further removed from the curriculum and more engaged in managerial/financial tasks and compliances. It may be the only chance they get to meaningfully engage in this space for the year – let them play!

The fun now begins as the curriculum is about to be mapped!

Mapping the curriculum

Step 1. Organise the staff to move into their teams and allocate spaces. (If the education support officers know their teams, they should join, too.)

Ideally, this will be in spaces where each conversation does not impose on another. The task of mapping the curriculum is challenging enough without competing noise (albeit productive) from another group. There may be temptations to engage in conversations with other nearby groups. This will only serve to have the thinking polluted by different thought patterns or ideas that others are working on.

Try as best as you can to keep all teams within a reasonable distance, too, though. Some schools consume a large footprint and spreading teams to all corners could be worthwhile for sound, but an impractical distance for leaders/specialists to travel. If there is a particular curriculum leader that needs to attend to each of the groups, the task may be beyond practical due to distance.

Step 2. Share that specialists and leadership teachers will be roving to support.

By sharing this, it will make everyone aware of the expectations and defuse any of the thinking that this is a task for classroom teachers only. By having a whole teaching staff (and possibly the education support officers), it allows for a consistent understanding of process, more ideas and thoughts being offered, and shows how each member of staff is valued equally.

Step 3. Have available the following documents in either print or digital.

These must be shared with everyone who will be participating. Toggling between tabs and documents can be as troublesome as using scissors and a glue stick. The most important thing is that everyone has everything they need and that everyone is following the process.

- **Student responses** – ensure that these are presented in a manner that shows what the students are interested in learning about and the ways in which they like to learn.
- **The curriculum templates** – these, as outlined previously, are the curriculum standards listed and colour coded. If they are to be cut and pasted from paper, then have multiple copies per group – one

for recording thoughts on or making note of which standards will be replicated across inquiries/years.

- **The scope and sequence of previous learning** – without these it could end up that curriculum is covered again by students who have previously engaged in it. While previous teachers may hold that information, or indeed curriculum leaders, having all of these in one document ensures that what is needed on the day is accessible and ready. Removing barriers and complexity is key.
- **A pre-made mapping document** – this document will act as the landing place for the mapped curriculum to be placed – this can be as simple as a large piece of butcher's paper for each of the macro concepts for the two-year cycle or a digital document ready to be populated.

Step 4. Reorient the staff to the macro concepts.

If staff do not have an understanding of what each macro concept (or term's) foci or broad direction is, then mapping is an act in futility. Staff, as discussed in Chapter 2, should have had time to own and understand the concepts and what scope for inquiries they may lead to. It is imperative to ensure that the staff know the broader thinking required and where to allocate curriculum standards.

The below is an example of a populated template for Grades 1 and 2 for one of the pre-identified macro concepts, in this case 'Identity & Humanity'. Note the second standard in the odd year is repeated in the even years (at the foot of the table). This would signify that this school wanted its students to cover this curriculum standard in both years.

Identity & Humanity	
Odd Years	**Even Years**
They examine messages related to health decisions and describe how to help keep themselves and others healthy, safe and physically active.	By the end of Level 2, students use and give examples of different kinds of questions.
They select strategies at home and/or school to keep themselves healthy and safe and are able to ask for help with tasks or problems.	Students express and describe thinking activity.
By the end of Level 2, students show an awareness of the feelings and needs of others.	They practise some learning strategies.
They identify and describe personal interests, skills and achievements and reflect on how these might contribute to school or family life.	Students demonstrate and articulate some problem-solving approaches.
They practise solving simple problems, recognising there are many ways to resolve conflict.	By the end of Level 2, students describe changes that occur as they grow older.
They describe given needs or opportunities.	They recognise how strengths and achievements contribute to identities.
Students identify and explain acts and situations that have ethical dimensions, using illustrative examples.	They examine messages related to health decisions and describe how to help keep themselves and others healthy, safe and physically active.
Students generate ideas that are new to them and make choices after considering personal preferences.	Students demonstrate positive ways to interact with others.
Students identify words that indicate components of a point of view.	They select strategies at home and/or school to keep themselves healthy and safe and are able to ask for help with tasks or problems.

Then the actual mapping begins. This requires the teams to disaggregate and reaggregate curriculum standards from each other and align them with an A and B sequence (could be easily called odd years or even years). We have all heard of the crowded curriculum or the overcrowded curriculum – a notion that at its very heart suggests that there is too much content to cover in the time allocated. Creating a clouded curriculum is a different notion altogether.

The clouded curriculum – we know the water cycle: water boils and turns into steam, then condenses again into water droplets. What we are doing through the process is not too dissimilar – the biggest difference is we are using many different starting points. Think of Science as one 'body of water', Digital Technologies as another, and each individual curriculum area and capability as a distinct body of water.

Naturally, when bodies of water exist, they are in a part of the water cycle. As soon as the temperature is right, water will naturally begin to evaporate. The hotter the temperature, the greater the rate of evaporation. So, if our collective knowledge and wisdom is the temperature in this model, the more we think, discuss and play, the greater the 'temperature'.

As the conversations develop and continue, bigger ideas begin to form and crystallise. This is when we have the clouded curriculum. Our 'water vapour' has begun to condense and form clouds. It is only now that we have a sense of the bigger picture can we begin to fit things together as well as the direction and 'shape' of the inquiry.

Repeating this cycle/process against all the broad areas that the curriculum is being divided into enables the school to have a skyline of learning with all the clouds.

The role of the curriculum leader or pedagogical leader(s)

While teams are working independently, this is when the curriculum/pedagogical leader(s) have to be agile, nimble and ready to challenge thinking. Having a depth of knowledge of what is in the curriculum at each level, knowing where the students have previously explored in their learning and the ability to work with teams to ensure accuracy, completeness and rigour is paramount. Their minds need to be in the moment and quickly adjust to accommodate different personalities, team dynamics and efficacies. It is one thing to set up the process – but being present in the process and actively driving it are different demands.

If teams are located with everyone within a short enough distance, the leader(s) can rove through and probe each group. Knowing what to look for, listen out for and ultimately challenge will be key to the role. There will be some teams that receive a disproportionate amount of time – but this process is about equity, not equality. Depending on their experience, confidence and diligence, each team will, at a different point, require different amounts of support, challenge or intervention.

Ultimately, they will need to be prepared to be flexible – but at the end of the day be prepared to ask a lot of questions and be ready to answer them, too!

Here are some possible considerations or occurrences on the day to look out for:

- Has the previous learning been considered?
- Has student voice been included or ignored?
- The team that finishes too soon
- The team that takes forever
- The individual that dominates the conversation
- The team that can't/won't do it without support
- The team that ignores the process
- The team that is thinking of previous units and maps the curriculum to suit what they are comfortable with
- If, for example, the Grade 1 and 2 teams are not working together, but they share a curriculum, should they work together to ensure greater transparency and collegiality in the process?

This may be the reality faced with many, none or all of the above. This is when the strength of the leadership team is crucial. If it is anticipated that a particular team may display certain behaviours, then nominate someone from the leadership team to start with them. It is not a divide and conquer leadership style, it is a support and challenge in context leadership style.

The role of specialists unpacked

When engaging in different groups, the ideal would be that they contribute on two fronts. The first is absolute support and help in mapping the curriculum; the second to view the mapping from their perspective, keeping an open mind as to how they could meaningfully integrate or support them learning in that inquiry through their specialist program.

At no point is it ever intended that a specialist teacher compromises their program for the sake of fitting in. Moreover, it is an encouragement that they find ways to connect with the learning and ensure the learning for students is less in silos and more connected. Keeping them involved at this stage ensures they can find meaningful links to their own program(s).

The role of leadership unpacked

Leadership that avails themselves of the opportunity to engage in this meaningful work will benefit from the experience as it allows them to potentially reconnect with curriculum. It also provides an opportunity for all staff to see leaders as doers, and as invested in the curriculum development and mapping as everyone else. One potential bonus is that leadership has the opportunity to witness the mechanisms and dynamics of the teams they have designed and placed together.

Mapping is 'complete' once all curriculum standards have been mapped against a theme/term over a two-year period. Should you only have time to map one year, then allocate the standards that will be looked at for that year. The remaining standards are those that will need to be mapped for the upcoming year.

Below is an image that demonstrates the full articulation of how curriculum can be mapped over a two-year period against six macro concepts:

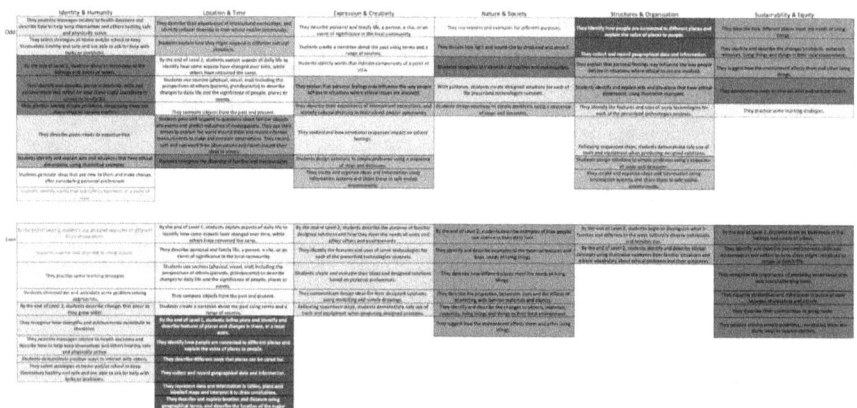

Reviewing the mapping

This is the point where the role of the curriculum/pedagogical leader, leadership team or working party come together and view the 'big picture' of the curriculum map. Being in the midst of this requires a high cognitive load and has the possibility of not being able to *see the forest for the trees*. Stepping back after the mapping process is completed is crucial in ensuring that there is clarity and any inconsistencies, variances and further considerations can be identified and shared back. The role will be to attend to the following:

- Audit that there is a reasonable distribution of learning standards across each area – this by no means equates to equality.
- Review and revisit whether the students have covered this learning previously – and if so, audit whether it is different and sophisticated enough to justify.
- Check to ensure that all curriculum standards are mapped and have a place over the one- or two-year cycle created.
- Analyse whether (if the curriculum is a two-year assessment period) there is clear delineation between grades within those levels – for example, have the Grade 3 and 4 teachers worked together or separately? If separate, have they mapped the same curriculum differently? Or is it similar enough to merge the units?
- Generate a list of questions, thoughts and prompts to provide the staff with by way of feedback.
- Consider how this will be presented to the staff for their feedback. Consider the forum and structure and also honour the significant efforts that have led to this point.

Could any of this be completed absenting the teacher from the process?

Absolutely it could. And the process is so much quicker and less complex. One coordinator or leader or even a faculty or team of leaders can attend to this task and liberate the load from the teachers. It allows for big picture thinking, leaving the how to the teachers. But is that what we want? Learning delivered to teachers and saying, "Here's one I made earlier." However, curriculum mapping is not an episode of *Play School*, nor is it *Blue Peter*.

But the question is, should it?

The process of delivering an already created package is disempowering and feels as though the important part of knowing and understanding the curriculum has been embezzled by others higher up. The more input, thinking and active participation teachers have in the mapping of the curriculum, the more they will understand it and actively follow it when implementing.

> *"Something happens when you feel ownership. You no longer act like a spectator or consumer, because you're an owner"*
> – Bob Goff (2014)

Beware of programs and companies that offer a pre-mapped curriculum or indeed prefabricated units. These units of work bear no relationship to context and while they advocate for saving time, they come at a cost that is far more than financial. The cost is ownership and understanding – and in today's educational climate, these are two elements we can ill afford to live without.

Invest in people – not programs.

Chapter summary

- Ensure that the staff has a singular and universal understanding of what curriculum mapping is.
- Honour student voice and their previous learning.
- Build and share a template ready for staff to use.
- Allocate staff roles in order to map the curriculum.
- The curriculum leader(s)/pedagogical leader(s) have a specific role to play.
- This is not the work of classroom teachers – it is the work of all staff involved in learning and teaching with students.
- Begin mapping.
- Consider how leaders will actively participate – rove, roam and review.
- Ensure that all curriculum is mapped and conduct a post-mapping review.

Reflection

SWOT analysis – a SWOT analysis is a great tool for strategically planning or identifying a range of factors that may have an impact. It can help you view issues or positions from differing perspectives.

- **Consider your Strengths:** What is working well? What are the positives? What is currently positive and good?
- **Consider your Weaknesses:** What are your blind spots? What is not working well? What could be improved on?
- **Consider the Opportunities:** These are generally external. What possibilities exist for change? What could be done? What are the possible positives you could generate?
- **Consider the Threats:** What problems could arise? What could go wrong? What would prevent or block your progress?

By using a SWOT analysis, it will provide you with the opportunity to explore the following issues. The benefit of completing the threats is it allows you to think about the possible blockers (and just about every staff has them) and plan for that. Going into a meeting having considered the possible roadblocks and planning for them can be incredibly effective.

Conduct a SWOT analysis on the following, or you may have a different consideration to analyse:

- The process currently used in your school for mapping curriculum
- The process outlined in this chapter
- Paper vs digital – which will work for us?
- Working in current year teams vs next year's teams

SWOT analyses

The process currently used in your school for mapping curriculum	
Strengths	Weaknesses
Opportunities	Threats

The process outlined in this chapter	
Strengths	Weaknesses
Opportunities	Threats

Paper vs digital – which will work for us?	
Strengths	Weaknesses
Opportunities	Threats

Working in current year teams vs next year's teams	
Strengths	Weaknesses
Opportunities	Threats

CHAPTER 4

FRAMING THE INQUIRIES

"Our job is too difficult and too beautiful to do alone"
– **Amelia Gambetti (2015)**

"To bring the pieces back together rediscover communication. That poetry that comes from the squaring off between and the circling is worth it. Finding beauty in the dissonance"
– Tool: 'Schism'

With the task of mapping the curriculum across the year (or two-year cycle) complete, attentions, efforts and cognition need to focus now on galvanising and framing these standards into inquiries. In the previous chapter, the notion of a 'clouded curriculum' was introduced. This chapter will explore how to develop units from standards that are grouped together into inquires that are worth exploring.

It may be prudent to point out that when engaging in this practice in the initial stages, it would be potentially highly advantageous to have all the staff select the same macro concept to explore. Pausing to reflect and share can ensure there is consistency of understanding, breadth of curriculum coverage and the opportunity to celebrate and acknowledge the incredible thinking and teamwork that it required to achieve this. This will be explored further in this chapter.

Having the staff oriented in the macro concept will set them up for a greater chance of success also. Inform them that the content and development process being undertaken aligns with one of the macro concepts. It is important that staff read and reread (or even better, have a copy in front of them) in order to place some parameters around their thinking. Failure to do this may lead to tangential explorations that will ultimately result in time and thinking spent in the wrong direction.

To explore the framing, this chapter will look at the following:
- The Structure of Knowledge model
- Concepts to frame
- Selecting the concepts
- Distilling a statement
- Playing with words – more than a pun
- Two ways to proceed

The Structure of Knowledge model

H Lynn Erickson's (2001) body of work surrounding a conceptual-based curriculum is the foundation for many subsequent works. Throughout this chapter we will explore how to use Erickson's model, 'The Structure of Knowledge'. Using The Structure of Knowledge, it helps move learning or framing of learning from content-based to generalised (conceptual). Content is bound and specific, and also necessary. Education has moved from the notion of teachers filling empty vessels or the imparting of knowledge to be learned – it is far more complex and sophisticated. But learning about specific content within a generalised context provides examples and tangible constructs in which to broaden thinking.

The Structure of Knowledge

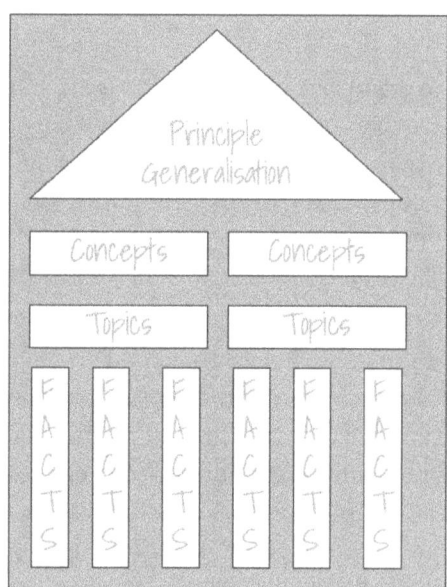

This model predicates that facts are the foundation of learning – this is the content. But to apply this framework, the facts don't need to be listed, as there are simply far too many to list. Imagine writing out and identifying every single morsel of learning that you could anticipate a student having at this stage (or any other) of planning.

In order to begin engaging with this model, it is a bottom-up approach beginning from topics. After having mapped your curriculum, you will know the 'facts' – they have already been allocated across the scope defined by your context. These will guide the thinking, not be the thinking.

Many schools now and in the past (and into the future) initially plan learning or inquires based on a topic. While this is not in and of itself a negative, it simply should not be the end point of the thought process. Indeed, starting with a topic can be extraordinarily supportive and generative; it just can't be the only piece of the puzzle. The topic is broad and is quite often the starting point for many professional planning sessions.

For illustrative purposes, we will use the example of light and sound.

The Structure of Knowledge

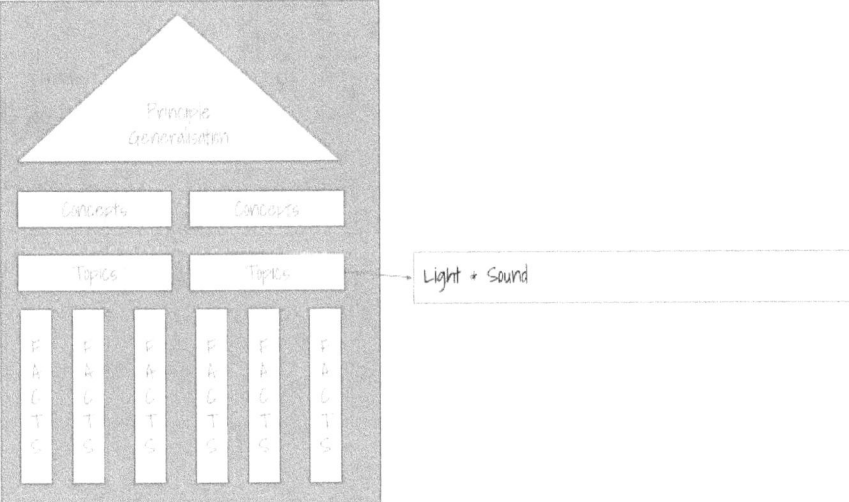

With a topic in place, the next step is to engage in dialogue to identify the concepts that underpin and will frame/guide the inquiry.

Concepts to frame

Once you have established your 'topic', then the next thing to consider is what concepts you want to frame your inquiry. There is no predetermined list of concepts that you can place in here, nor are there right or wrong answers. There are only going to be concepts that you identify to steer the learning. A quick search on the internet for a list of concepts reveals there is an abundance of them. Selecting the most appropriate ones is the element of this that requires careful consideration, conversation and deliberation.

Think of concepts at this point as a lens in which to view the learning. The lenses we are most familiar with are lenses within glasses – and they serve a handy analogy. If I put on my glasses, they sharpen my vision; if I put on my sunglasses, they block out UV and make everything appear darker and not as sharp; if I put on my wife's glasses, then everything just gets a little warped and blurry; if I put on my prescription sunglasses, it sharpens and darkens while blocking UV.

No matter which pair of glasses I have put on, the object I am viewing has not changed. But my ability to see it has. The different lenses send different messages to my brain to process and interpret the incoming stimuli differently. And this is the role that concepts play in shaping and framing the inquiries.

After living and working in Scotland, a leaving gift from the school community I worked in was a quaich. I had no idea what it was, what it symbolised or the significance of it. When I looked at it through my limited lenses, I could only work out it was a silver bowl with some Celtic patterns. But from others' lenses they knew all the different meanings and symbolisms, because of their frame of reference. This framing through lenses is highly powerful in influencing perceptions and approaches we take.

A traditional Scottish quaich

The following diagrams illustrate how the same topic can be viewed and articulated so very differently through the power of concept selection. This is using content from the junior years.

The Structure of Knowledge

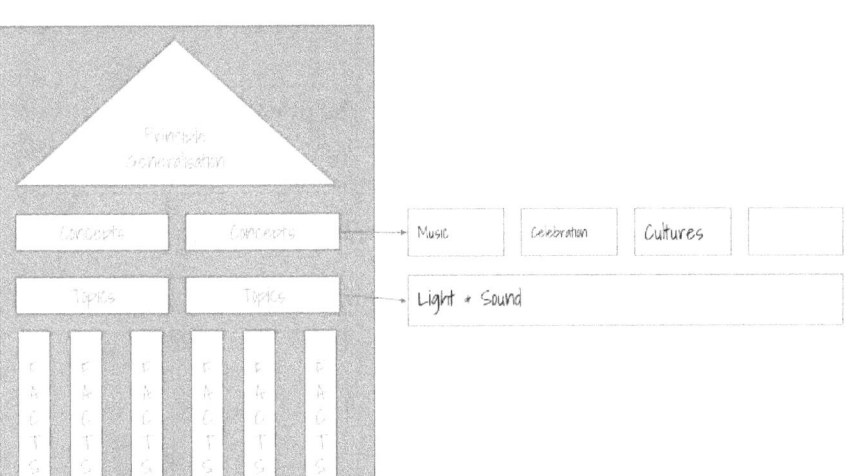

The Structure of Knowledge

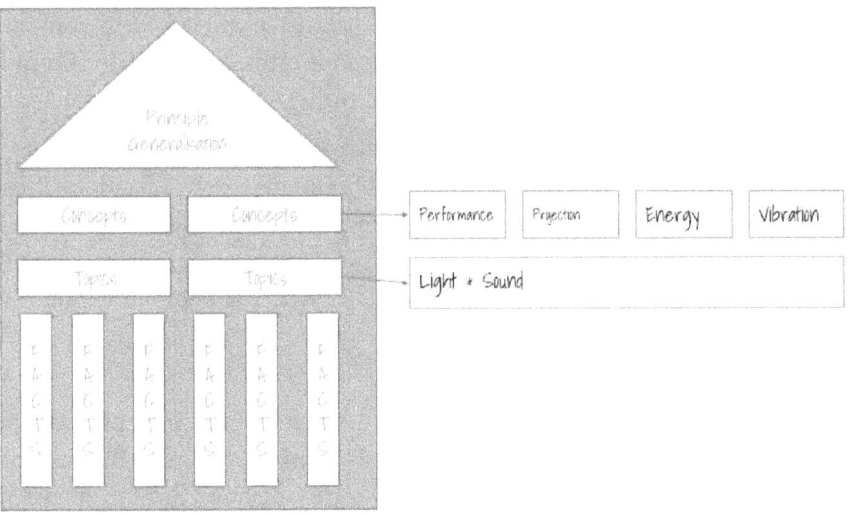

Framing the inquiries 53

Selecting the concepts

The examples on the previous page outline how different an inquiry can be through the use of concepts (this time playing the role of lenses). They don't serve to tweak or shuffle an inquiry through a micro adjustment; the learning isn't slightly askew. The learning is fundamentally altered as is the course of the inquiry. (Little Easter egg – google *askew* and check out the alignment of your page!)

There is no right or wrong in this instance. The ones you select are just that, the ones you select. A simple exercise is to, with the collaborative planning team, have each person independently record their own 'Top 5' concepts. After recording, have each of them share back. Record on butcher's paper or a whiteboard for everyone to see and tally any that are repeated. If there are any words that are close to each other in meaning, perhaps aggregate them. Looking at the collective thinking of the room, it now comes time to refine and select the concepts that will be the direction the unit heads in. The dominant voice in the room shouldn't be allowed to dominate, nor should that of the leader/facilitator. The thinking of the room is there, question what is a unique outlier. It may end up being the best one. Question them all, don't just accept that three out of five said it, so it makes the cut. Be discerning, be critical, just don't be challenging for the sake of it.

The concepts selected are varied and will change the direction of your inquiry. Like a filter on Snapchat or Instagram, it really can and does change what you see. Have a conversation with the team, encourage everyone to record their own concepts they believe will drive the unit and compare or work collaboratively from the outset. It is important to ensure there is ownership and understanding at this point, not agreeance and compliance.

As can be seen in the previous examples, the model has yet to be completed. Now comes the point where we develop the 'Principle Generalisation'. These always (as per the model) begin with the sentence starter: 'The student understands that...' The way to arrive at these is through acknowledgement of the concepts and the topic. The task for teachers here is to finish off that sentence stem while trying to fit at least one concept in (two or three make it stronger) and honouring the topic itself.

The first example for 'Light and Sound', using the concepts music, **celebration** and **cultures,** can lead us to the principle generalisation that 'Students understand that... **cultures celebrate** differently through light and sound.' While the word 'music' isn't explicitly referenced, it need not be. 'Cultures' and 'celebrate' are included in the 'final statement' on the model and make for a neatly composed sentence. And if we wanted to include music? It could read '**Cultures celebrate** through **music** and light' or '**Music** and light support **cultural celebrations**' or '**Celebrations** include **music** and light' or '**Cultural music** and celebrations are connected'. Each of these examples are valid, but this is where your context and direction come in. Choose well!

The second example, using the concepts **performance**, projection, energy and vibration, can lead to the principle generalisation that 'students understand that... light and sound enhance **performances**'. Picking up on one concept has shifted the focus of this inquiry dramatically (at the time of writing, I wanted to delete this pun, but since thought better of it). But it could read very differently again if a different concept was called to centre stage (apologies). If the concept projection was picked up, it could be interpreted in many ways. Is it a projection of voice or a projection of sound or light? The principle generalisation could well read 'Students understand that... light and sound can be **projected**'.

Both inquiries include the topic of light and sound – but they are so different. And that is great! As I mentioned earlier, the concepts you choose need to be the ones you want. In these two cases, they have provided the scope for very different learning. Neither is better than the other – they are simply different.

Work from topic to concept and eventually up to principle generalisation, but what comes next now that there is a sentence that starts 'Students understand that...'? By simply removing the sentence starter you may well have your finished product. Sometimes these statements will stand alone and be a perfect fit. For example, 'Cultures celebrate differently through light and sound' OR 'Light and sound enhance performances'.

There are some who believe auxiliary verbs such as is, be, have, has, etc, should be banned. I used to subscribe to this belief vehemently, but my stance has softened – but not too much. The belief is that by having those sorts of words in the statement, it becomes a closed statement and a fact. And if something is a fact, it has less capacity to be inquired into. The statement needs to be true, but not necessarily a fact. Using the light and sound example from above, it may read something like: 'Light and sound are produced by vibrations'.

All those statements can be used to proceed to refining the statements, but you need to select the ones most appropriate for the inquiry itself. Taking into consideration the cohort, the curriculum and the direction that the inquiry could go must be considered when deciding on which principle generalisation to move forward with.

The one thing these statements do not do is burrow down to a specific time or place. As they are conceptually developed, they do not reference events or people specifically. If I was studying Diwali or the Toro Nagashi (Japanese Lantern Festival), the learning explored would be limited to these specific examples. With a statement like 'Cultures celebrate differently through light and sound', it leaves scope for exploring these and others. It also allows for students to explore.

The following demonstrates how you may begin with a singular event and move from specific content to a generalised way of viewing. This is a different approach but still arrives at the same destination and a lot of the same characteristics.

Picking up on a recent event that is getting media coverage is a great way to make learning in the classroom real. But if you plan in advance for a 'topic', you don't have scope to address it. And if you plan with historical events, you run the risk of not being flexible enough to include current events. Generalisations just work so well for this. Here's how they work…

Take the following two examples of possible content that could be exclusively studied in an inquiry:

Questions	Content	Content
When	2011	79CE
Who	Citizens of Japan	Citizens of Pompeii
What	Japanese earthquake and tsunami	Volcanic eruption
Why	Situated on a fault line	Mount Vesuvius erupted
Summarised	In 2011, there was an earthquake and tsunami in Japan.	In 79CE, there was a volcanic eruption in Pompeii.
Impact	Lives of the people in Japan were impacted.	Lives of the people in Pompeii were impacted.

If we were to operate in the content-driven learning sphere, the learning could be summarised as such: 'In 2011, there was an earthquake and tsunami in Japan' or 'In 79CE, there was a volcanic eruption in Pompeii'.

These are locked in time, place, people and singular reasons. It is extremely unlikely that any inquiry is purely about this highly specified focus (although inquiries have been known to explore events such as gold rush, particular conflicts/battles or key events in history. The challenge now is how does the thinking transition and broaden the scope of learning? By generalising it!

Moving forward with the Japanese tsunami and earthquake example, I will demonstrate how to generalise and move away from content. 'But the tsunami *was* in Japan in 2011.' Sadly, that is correct. Broadening the thinking from the specific is *what* is required. Instead of focusing on 2011, the *when* needs to be expanded. The simplest way is to make it more timeless and general (less specific). The same thinking can be applied for *Who*, *What* and *Why* to complete the transition from content-driven to generalised thinking.

The table below illustrates the transition or differentiation between content-driven learning and a generalised approach to learning:

Questions	Content	Generalised
When	2011	At any time
Who	Citizens of Japan	People
What	Japanese earthquake and tsunami	Natural disasters
Why	Situated on a fault line	Natural forces
Summarised	In 2011, there was an earthquake and tsunami in Japan.	At any time, people can experience natural disasters due to natural forces.
Impact	Lives of the people in Japan were impacted.	People's lives are impacted by natural disasters

To summarise the learning when generalised, it would be: 'At any time, people can experience natural disasters due to natural forces.'

This leads to potential scope and broadening of the learning. It also offers the opportunity for teachers, should they wish to use an exemplar or model the learning the chance to. How rich would the learning be if the teacher was able to scaffold, work through, think aloud, model all the inquiry skills needed using the example of the Japanese tsunami or Pompeiian eruption with a view to having students engage in the content or launch into their own personal inquiries on within the scope of the generalised statement?!

Framing the inquiries

But the generalised statement is crude and unpolished; this is when it can be refined it and staff engage in a high stakes game of semantics.

At any time, people can experience natural disasters due to natural forces. Using this as the basis, the thinking needs to begin with the sentence starter (borrowing this from The Structure of Knowledge model – *The students understand that...* This is where teachers begin to craft a statement that will become the enduring understanding desired for the learners.

Let's put that into action – *The students understand that... at any time, people can experience natural disasters due to natural forces.* But you want these statements to be a bit shorter and capture the essence of the learning in as few, yet powerful, words as possible. I know gin is currently experiencing a renaissance of sorts, so we'll borrow from this world and distil.

Distilling a statement

Distilling is the process of extracting the essential meaning of something or the most important parts. When distilling gin, it takes heat and uses a lot of energy in the form of sugar. Distilling these types of statements will require heat in the form of questions, not accepting mediocrity or shortcut thinking, and takes a lot of energy (perhaps have some sugary treats on standby). The process is robust and rigorous and can become an exercise in semantics, and so it should. The meaning of words is so important.

After this process is complete, it could be distilled down to an essence: 'Natural disasters disrupt lives and livelihoods'.

A statement like this is transferable across time and age. Any school classroom in the world, no matter the age, students could engage in an inquiry into this statement. Younger learners may need more unpacking with certain elements and the depth of learning would vary (as it rightly should), but it can be inquired into. It is broad and generalised and can lead to many different avenues of learning. If this was the enduring understanding that was selected, a teacher could now use the Japanese tsunami example under the broader generalised statement. With the right guidance and learning culture in a classroom, a student could inquire into any other natural disaster and know they are operating within a broad area of learning. They could explore Pompeii as a personal inquiry under this statement.

As mentioned previously, this is a high stakes game in semantics. There is an elegance in selecting the 'right' words and knowing that at a word level, there is potential for an inquiry or learning opportunity. Taking a closer look at the statement again, there are two distinct linguistic patterns that present themselves for inquiry (or at least potential inquiry).

Playing with words – more than a pun

Before continuing, reread the sentence and see if your inquiring mind identifies the two potential inquiries at a word level, not just a statement one:

Natural disasters disrupt lives and livelihoods.

Whether you identified them or not, the act of engaging in learning is the important aspect. It so happens that in this statement, there are the following word level elements that can be inquired into:

Natural disasters disrupt **live**s and **live**lihoods.

- Lives and livelihoods

Both have 'live' in them. What is the difference semantically? What is the difference in meaning? Both have the base word of live in them, but different suffixes. For those who, like me, love playing in this space, then I'd encourage you to explore the work of Neil Ramsden (www.neilramsden.co.uk/spelling/matrix/index.html).

Natural **dis**asters **dis**rupt lives and livelihoods.

- Disasters and disrupt

Both words have the prefix 'dis' in them. Students could inquire into what 'dis' (not) means as a prefix. Then the other two words are bound morphemes – what could they mean? 'Rupt' can be found in disrupt, rupture, corrupt, abrupt – and it simply means *to break*. Aster on the other hand relates to star/planet.

Think about this last part – **dis**-aster. Something so big that the stars are not aligned or on your side. Literally so **dis**-astrous that the entire universe seems to be working against you! It certainly brings a new meaning to the stars aligned… and perhaps not winning the football match isn't actually a disaster – more of a disappointment!

Selecting different words in that statement would alter the meaning, even when using synonyms, as each word has a precise purpose and meaning. There are a lot of words in the English language, so we have many choices. So please, choose carefully and be considered in your word choice.

Two ways to proceed

Once you have created your first statement, there are two logical ways to proceed. They are:

- Pause the process and review collectively.
- Continue the process and complete it for the other macro concepts.

Let's explore the first option and **'Pause the process and review collectively'**.

If all teams across the school have engaged in the same macro concept and created their singular statement, this provides the opportunity to see how similar and different the thinking across the school is.

- What if two teams have the same or very similar statement?

Grab the popcorn and sit back and watch the fireworks! Please don't! But you do want to ensure that there are rigorous and professional conversations occurring. Someone may have to play the role of pacifier, pragmatist, protagonist or pugilist. Ultimately, the conversations have to come back to what is appropriate given the curriculum accountabilities that each team has. If there is a clear reason for one to be chosen over the other, then there isn't really a disagreement that can stand up. Curriculum wins, not personality.

If in the strange instance there is a case to be made for both, then it requires a certain degree of trust and professionalism to engage in the conversation. It may be the case that two statements are centred on the same broad theme, for example, sustainability. The Grade 1s and Grade 5s may both come up with statements that read fairly similarly. The effort to arrive at these statements has not been without significant amounts of cognitive function – so honour that. Be clear that both are valid, but if they are too similar, they need to tweak them.

Perhaps the Grade 1s are more about water and how we can be more sustainable, and the Grade 5s are more focused on sustainable energy production. Encourage them to go back to the concepts and play with trialling either a different one or leaving one out and see what happens. It may be that a leader will have to get down there and have pencil and paper and toil with them to graft a new one.

The other tact is to reorient the staff in the macro concept and its definition. Ask the staff to reflect and justify how their statement 'fits under' that macro concept. This will ensure that they are conscious of the bigger picture and that they haven't gone too far off on a tangent. Or if they have, it provides them the opportunity to realign themselves with the required umbrella.

Continue the process and complete it for the other macro concepts until you have a fully articulated scope of learning across the school.

Now let's explore the second option and **'Continue the process and complete it for the other macro concepts'**.

This process allows teams to dedicate time in the same headspace without coming up for air and checking in with other teams. The benefits of this are that you can get into a groove and be highly productive. Teams can, when left to continue, benefit from the dedicated time. This should ensure that they are mapping out their year with big statements and they are all next to each other in one space to ensure they have no conflict within their own team.

When it is all done and dusted and each team has chosen their statements and there is no conflict, go visual and go big. Have the team record their statements on A3 paper (as seen below) and lay out the year. It will serve to give the whole staff a broader understanding of the learning across the year.

Example of recorded statements on A3 paper

Displaying them in this way allows for the ability to be viewed by year level and by macro concept. Invite questions from other teams, have people sell their ideas to others and make it a bit of an exercise in thinking. When it is all over, move them to a central space (staffroom or professional learning space) and invite further feedback and commentary/questions on the statements displayed. Imagine that – a staff of inquirers!

At some timely point, the feedback and refining needs to stop as you need to commit to finalising the process and commit to the statements themselves.

Consider the ownership and rigour that has gone into their development. Each and every staff member has a sense of ownership and has been an active player in the game of development. This sense of ownership can only serve to set a staff up for success.

Chapter summary

- Engage in rich and robust practices in dialogue when establishing the essential learning for each inquiry.
- Principle generalisations, as developed in The Structure of Knowledge, are broader than content and provide scope for learning beyond curriculum.
- Choose your words carefully as each word has a meaning and a connotation that will shift the focus of learning.
- Decide on a process for the development of your statements.
- Think of these statements like a fraction – try to simplify them as much as possible.
- Articulate the year both across the concept and the grade.
- Review the learning across the concept and the grade – debate and decide.

Reflection

Think about a recent inquiry you have been involved in (either as a leader, teacher or as a learner). What was the enduring understanding for the learners?

- **Was it made explicit to the students?** If it was, how was this done? If it wasn't, why not?
- **Was it displayed?** Was this up on a wall in a classroom? Was it in a centralised space? Did other members of the school/school community have access to know the learning?
- **What was your word choice?** If you had a shared enduring understanding, what was the process for the structuring/word choice like?
- **If you didn't have one...** What would it have been? Are there any key words you would have intentionally included? How would you develop it?

CHAPTER 5

STARTING WITH A QUESTION IS QUESTIONABLE

"One learns by asking questions, not by answering them"
– Peter Drucker (2015)

"I want to free the beast from its cage…
make it all worth something"
– **Montaigne: 'I'm a Fantastic Wreck'**

In different schools there are different ways that inquiries are presented to students. Some have titles, some have questions, some have statements, some none or all of the above. While each have their reasoning, this chapter will explore the thinking behind why starting with a statement is the most powerful and empowering way to present an inquiry.

As teachers, we like to play with words – whether it is alliteration, rhyme or clever puns (some of the most cringeworthy and synchronously glorious work has happened here). These are particularly present when we design titles for inquiries. I recall spending almost as long thinking of a title than we did for planning during more than one planning session. What was it for? We did it so we could have a title that encapsulated the essence of the unit and was 'catchy' for the students. Ultimately, our time would have been better invested in planning for the learning, rather than the title.

To explore the notion of questioning and how to start an inquiry, this chapter is broken into the following sections:

- What have we done?
- Knowledge vs understanding
- The hidden message behind questions

- Taking the learning pulse
- Question types
- Questions are the drivers

What have we done?

Our units based on the human body and body systems was given the title 'Body Whys'. See what we did there?! While it had a nice play on words, it was an opportunity lost. I don't to this day remember what I taught specifically, but I remember the title. I worry that the students, too, walked away remembering the title more than the essential message that was behind the inquiry.

In an inquiry focusing on multiculturalism, we dubbed that inquiry 'Culture Mulcher'. Some lovely rhyming again. Mercifully, this one came quickly and we could move on to planning the unit. But we dutifully went back to our respective classrooms and made a display that had most prominently the title: Culture Mulcher. What was the key thing we wanted the students to learn?

- That their teachers were quite witty and could come up with a 'catchy' title?
- That the most important thing to learn was that there was a thing called a 'culture mulcher'?
- That our displays focused on the witty work we created?
- Or could it have been around the underlying concepts we wished to impart to the students around multiculturalism and harmony?

And the classic – feathers, fur, scales and skin. While it does act as a good mnemonic and catchphrase, it does beg the question: Was the essential learning that sat behind those words gained? Could it have been better? (Yes, it could have been.)

Knowledge vs understanding

There is a significant difference between knowing and understanding. It is pretty easy these days, with the support of ChatGPT, Google Bard and other emerging AI platforms to demonstrate knowledge and create synthetic understanding. I can simply ask a question or provide a stimulus and it will produce a more than sound response – and quickly. But does it understand or just know? And what is the difference? And then does the user actually know or understand? Do they simply copy and paste and pass it off as their own with some tweaks along the way? Either way, this is not my definition of understanding.

The best way to witness understanding is through the teaching of others. Once you know the content well enough to explain it to someone else, that is understanding. One conjecture I have is understanding can be a simple mathematical equation. Without any knowledge it is impossible to have application, therefore, there can be no understanding. There is a definite and tangible correlation between the two. If your knowledge level is non-existent, and you attempt to apply in four different contexts, it cannot occur. In mathematical terms, it can be represented as 0×4. This equation is always going to result in 0. Just like 0 multiplied by anything will give you the same answer: 0.

The same can be said about knowledge and application. The more knowledge there is and the more applications you have for it, the greater the end result. The product of this equation is understanding. *Knowledge × Application = The Level of Understanding*. Harpaz (2005) describes this as, "...thinking acts upon knowledge in order to bring it into the mind; when that operation succeeds, understanding is achieved."

Similarly, the inverse is without application, there is no knowledge. Learners cannot gain an understanding without having the skills to apply or store their knowledge. Knowledge is useless unless it is utilised. Having a garage full of tools in which to build the second storey is useless if you have no idea how to use them. They will sit around and gather dust. The person with all the tools could invite people around to look at their tools to show them off in an attempt to impress. Should they attempt to use the tools, it could result in a disastrous failure (but it would be an attempt all the same). The second storey may never materialise and if it does, may not be a firm or solid structure. More than likely, it will have structural flaws and holes in it. In the right hands these tools can be used masterfully and impressively, but to someone who doesn't know how to use them... dangerous and ultimately ineffective.

As the dependent learner develops and gains in knowledge, they are able to use this knowledge and apply it to different situations. Gaining in application allows for the maintenance of a level of knowledge to occur (if deep understanding is to be gained). The emergent (or transitory) learner has a blend of skills that allow for transition into the independent stage.

The independent learner is as Gardner (1989) describes the master or disciplinary expert.

Here's a practical example demonstrating the difference between knowledge and understanding...

> **Teacher:** Who thinks they can answer two questions for me? One you are just about guaranteed to be right and the other, you've got a really good chance of being wrong.
>
> **Student:** I can.
>
> **Teacher:** Great, come out the front for me, so we can all see and hear you answer these.
>
> **Student:** OK.
>
> **Teacher:** Your first question, which I can just about 100% guarantee you will get right is coming, are you ready? And no, that wasn't your question.
>
> **Student:** Yup, I think I am.
>
> **Teacher:** Just remember that the second one is tricky. But it is related, so there's a little clue for you. Here comes your first question.
>
> **Student:** All right.
>
> **Teacher:** If I looked outside at the sky, in the middle of the day, and there wasn't a cloud in the sky, what colour would the sky be?
>
> **Student:** Blue.
>
> **Teacher:** Perfect! I knew you would get that one, but that was the easy one. Are you ready for your second one that is way harder and you might just get wrong?
>
> **Student:** Sort of.
>
> **Teacher:** Here it comes. No googling or using the internet in any way to help you. Why is the sky blue?
>
> **Student:** Is it something to do with the reflection of the ocean up to the sky?
>
> **Teacher:** Are you giving an answer or asking a question?
>
> **Student:** It was a question. I think it is because the sun shines down onto the ocean and that reflects back up onto the sky and makes it blue.

The reasons are significantly more complex than this and lie in the reflection of light as it passes through the Earth's atmosphere. But, as can be witnessed, it is far easier to demonstrate knowledge of a topic, than it is to display understanding. It requires more effort and intentionality to develop this with our students. Surely the main focus of an inquiry (or indeed any other learning) should be that of understanding. There is a case for knowing your multiplication facts with automaticity, but if you have no notion of what 8 × 4 actually looks like or means, then you are simply parroting facts.

My contention is that you start your inquiry with a statement that can be inquired into; not a question that requires answering. Through this inquiring the understanding has potential, and with careful and strategic support and planning, can flourish.

The hidden message behind questions

Education has been championing the case for problem solvers; but could this be an inadequate shortcoming? I posit as a counterpoint there is a case for desiring students to be problem finders, not just problem solvers. Therefore, we are creating students who are 'problem literate'. By providing a question at the start of the unit, while we may be modelling questioning, we are also modelling something far more unintentionally dismissive – that my questions matter more.

If we present students with questions, the messages received really are:

- My question is far more important than yours.
- Here is the learning I need you to do.
- I've done the hard work of thinking of a question, now it is over to you to find the answer I am seeking.
- While you may be inquirers (or at least that is what I think I'm trying to make you), ultimately, you are researchers.
- It is a long version of the game 'Guess the answer in my head'.

Put your questions away and let the students ask them. Students are naturally inclined to ask them, so let them. Sir Ken Robinson (2006), in his seminal Ted Talk, talks of how schools crush creativity; some of this creativity is questioning. It is only through the traditional education process that we find our students lose heart and become passive learners. This stultification cannot continue and can be simply eradicated to frame an inquiry through flipping the question to a statement – one worthy of the students' energies and efforts to inquire into.

How could you go about assessing these statements as the inquiry progresses?

Taking the learning pulse

Visible Learning Flipped – imagine you didn't share the learning intention on a lesson. Many Hattie fans will be tempted to take a match to this page – feel free to burn after reading. Imagine that you asked the students at the end of the lesson: What do you think the learning I wanted you to get out of the lesson was? That would be such a good gauge or exit ticket to fathom how effective your lesson was in hitting the mark, and it would provide insight into individual acquisition.

Now scale up to the inquiry. If you planned the statement you want the students to inquire into, hide it away and don't share it. Keep it in your planner, not on your walls or screens, but actively keep it in your minds and plan with it at the forefront of your thinking. At the end of the week, you could have your students speculate (or hypothesise or state) what they believe the statement is. This could be done individually, in small groups or as a whole class. The benefit of operating at an individual level here is that you will gain insights on individual understanding – but your context and age of your students should be considered.

By simply providing five minutes of reflection time, you could gain such rich and powerful insights into student understanding and the effectiveness of the direction you have travelled in the inquiry. Take an inquiry focusing on the statement: *Rules and laws can promote or deny equality.*

Say, after a week of learning experiences, your students provide the following responses:

- Rules are there to keep us safe.
- Rules are important.
- Laws are made by governments.
- Laws and rules are different.
- You need to follow laws more than rules.
- Schools have rules.

The insight that this provides is quite profound. There is no mention of how laws or rules promote or deny equality. That would tell me as a teacher that my focus has to shift to make sure more learning experiences are developed to cover this. This may simply be as a result of that was all you covered, and you can rest assured in the knowledge that the rest would be covered. But if you had covered the 'equality' element, it provides you, as a responsive educator, an opportunity.

What a rich insight to both student learning and effectiveness of your teaching. The table below demonstrates how you could track student learning and teaching over the course of an inquiry:

	I think this inquiry is getting me to understand that...
Week 1	
Week 2	
Week 3	
Week 4	
Week 5	
Week 6	
Week 7	

Here is what a completed version could look like, using the 'rules and laws' example:

	I think this inquiry is getting me to understand that...
Week 1	Rules make us safe.
Week 2	Laws are there to protect us.
Week 3	Rules and laws are different.
Week 4	People are treated differently in different countries.
Week 5	Rules and laws make a difference.
Week 6	Some rules and laws aren't fair.
Week 7	Rules and laws should be fair.

Deconstructing this, I would speculate that the teaching has followed a sequence that looks like the following:

	Rules	Laws	Rules and laws are related	Impact of rules and laws	Promoting or denying quality
Week 1	✓				
Week 2		✓			
Week 3	✓	✓	✓		
Week 4				✓	
Week 5				✓	
Week 6				✓	
Week 7				✓	✓

It would appear through this analysis that the statement was taught almost from left to right. But if you want understanding, not just surface knowledge, you can't leave such an important aspect to the last week to ensure coverage. Also, this would be indicative of a teacher who is still in control of the learning experiences and providing little to no time for personal inquiries. What an insight you could gain. This is student voice screaming at the top of its lungs – listen to me – this is what I am getting out of the lessons. And your response should be like that of Ground Control from NASA (and David Bowie): We can hear you, Major Tom.

If taking the pulse every week is too frequent, then spread it out – capture the feedback and thinking every fortnight. There is no rule around the frequency, though doing this daily may well become tiresome and ultimately disengaging. Leaving it to the end of the inquiry (or larger gaps) may not leave you with any (or enough) time to respond to the direction of the learning.

But if your students are the ones asking the questions, where do they get their modelling of what a good question is? What questions are worth asking? They will defer to their environment (as a general rule) and copy those around them that ask the questions. If you model good questioning, there is a better chance of your students asking good questions.

Question types

There are different ways to view questions: open, closed, shallow, deep, rich, thick, thin, etc. Each question has a time and a place, but which area do you, as a teacher, find yourself asking the most questions? If they are closed, then you will probably get short answers and in time only be asked closed questions to answer yourself from your students. The types of questions that I have witnessed, as a teacher, student and coach, are directive, learning, open and closed. These four occur in each classroom setting, whether they are generated by teacher or student. The quantity of questions varies, but invariably all questions can be assigned to these categories.

- **Directive questions:** These are questions that give directions, but not about learning. Can you please put that down? Is that what you are supposed to be doing? Is there any chance you could please stop calling out? Why did you push him?
- **Learning-based questions:** These types of questions are pretty self-explanatory. They are focused on learning. Is there a different way to express that? Have you checked your answer? I wonder what would happen if you answered that differently? What makes you think/say that?
- **Open questions:** These by their very definition are open to interpretation. There is no set answer or predetermined direction or response. Offering these questions leaves the space to generate a vast range of answers.
- **Closed questions:** These questions mean they have a definitive answer. There really isn't any grey here, just right or wrong. They absolutely have a place in our repertoire, but they won't generate variances in correctness.

A simple auditing tool is analysing the questions you and your students ask during the school day (or even a lesson). Using a matrix, as seen below, have a peer audit the types of questioning you model. All they need to do is record tally marks in the appropriate quadrants:

Teacher	Directive	Learning
Open		
Closed		

Student	Directive	Learning
Open		
Closed		

You may be surprised by the results of where the majority of your questions lie. Depending on the purpose of the question (and the session), it will determine the type of questioning. But the type of teacher you are and the type of questions you ask will determine engagement levels in answers (or students generating their own questions). A classic scene from *Ferris Bueller's Day Off* (1986) sees a class full of disengaged students subjected to closed questions. For those unfamiliar, here's the transcript...

> *"In 1930 in the Republican controlled House of Representatives, in an effort to alleviate the effects of... Anyone? Anyone? The Great Depression*
>
> *Passed the... Anyone? Anyone? The tariff bill. The Holly-Smoot Tariff Act*
>
> *Which...? Anyone? Raised or lowered? Raised tariffs in an effort to collect more revenue for the federal government*
>
> *Did it work? Anyone? Anyone know the effects? It did not work and the United States sank deeper into the Great Depression*
>
> *Today, we have a similar debate over this. Anyone know what this is? Class? Anyone? Anyone? Anyone seen this before? The Laffer curve*
>
> *Anyone know what this says? It says that at this point on the revenue curve you will get exactly the same amount of revenue as at this point. This is very controversial.*
>
> *Does anyone know what Vice President Bush called this in 1980? Anyone? Something-d-o-o economics. Voodoo economics."*

This transcript demonstrates three things worth highlighting:

1. This teacher either wanted closed questions or had no ability to ask different types.
2. The students were so disengaged that the teacher answered all the questions.
3. That is a rapid-fire of 18 questions in such a short amount of time!

Using that quadrant, all of these questions can be placed in the bottom-right quadrant – which is not where you will get buy-in generally. This is a space that is very teacher-led and although it is about learning, the question is how much learning is going on.

In reality, over the course of a lesson, session or day, you will find your questions are in all four quadrants, and the hope is that your students will achieve the same. But the vast majority should be in the upper-right quadrant – as this is where dialogue, interaction and learning occur most frequently.

With the notion of asking good questions being in the upper-right quadrant, the task now becomes to present your class with a statement that can be inquired into and good questions asked of it. As if you lead with a good question, you may well just get back good answers – there's nothing wrong with that. But surely having students be adept at asking questions and answering them is far more powerful, empowering and engaging than simply answering.

If you do this and set a personal goal, then please 'pull back the curtain' and be transparent with your students. Let them in on the goal you've set. We know that young students are great at not having filters sometimes, and they will keep you more accountable than yourself sometimes. So, let them know you are changing your questioning technique because they will pay close attention and let you know when you have asked the ones you are after.

Better yet, explicitly show them the grid (this is age dependent, but a case can be made for doing it with any age group) and have them keep you accountable. What a sense of rich empowerment the students would feel if they help keep you accountable for your learning. This flipping of the norm can only work to enhance student engagement.

Questions are the drivers

An inquiry without questions is not an inquiry. In order to establish that the inquiry is actually all about questioning, set it up from the start to let the students ask questions. Etymologically speaking, it makes a lot of sense. 'In' coming from the Proto-Indo European language *en* meaning in, and the Latin *quaerere* meaning 'ask' or 'seek' placed together give us 'in asking or in seeking,' or as we know it, 'inquiry'. Isn't that what good learning or a good inquiry is? Nowhere in the origin of the word does it say relate at all to researching or answering. If it was, we would certainly not use the word inquiry.

There is a reasonable chance we would have a new word. This neologism would be something like: *In answering* as its meaning. Starting with the 'in' (same as above), but we would need to apply the word *swerian* (which is where we derive the *swer* part of answer. Therefore, our new word would be *inswer*. And we would have students engaging in *inswering*, not inquiring. There is a huge difference.

But we don't do *inswery* because we want our students to ask questions, to seek – to inquire.

Chapter summary

- Presenting a statement is more powerful than a question.
- Developing inquirers, not answerers, is what we are seeking.
- Audit the learning through questions in order to establish how the focus of your teaching is in direct relationship to the learning of your students.
- Consider how value-laden your questions are at present.
- Audit your questioning in order to ensure the students are modelled the 'right type' of questions.
- Use questions to drive learning.

Reflection

Have a peer conduct an audit on you or conduct a self-audit (this is trickier to do, though). Or, as a team, rotate through and audit each other to see what sort of questioning is happening in your learning spaces.

Teacher	Directive	Learning
Open		
Closed		

	Directive	Learning
Student		
Open		
Closed		

Be brave and share what you have seen in your own practice, own what your current reality is. Be vulnerable and share the results with peers, set a goal and have a focus on asking different types of questions.

After you have set a goal, give yourself a good period of time, around one or two weeks, and conduct the audit again. With an intentioned and dedicated focus to changing your questioning, hopefully it is evident in your data.

It will take longer for the types of questions the students ask to change. That is OK. Reward, praise, celebrate and make a big show of any questions that students ask that fall in the top-right quadrant. Make it something worth aiming for.

CHAPTER 6

BREAKING IT DOWN INTO SMALLER PARTS

"A strong curriculum is one of the foundations of any quality education system"
– **Department of Education, Australian Government**

"It's just a lot, it's just a lot. I wanna care for all the little things I got"
– **K.Flay: 'It's Just a Lot'**

I'm a fan of pizza. I love it. Aside from the debate about a circular food being placed in a square box being cut into triangles, it is just delicious. But have you ever tried eating a pizza without it being cut into slices? As a recovered male teenager, I can confirm that it is messy and challenging. Just holding the pizza is quite hard work, balancing it, working out a starting point, general etiquette, the list goes on and on.

There is a really good reason that pizza is cut into slices. Common sense!

That is exactly what this chapter will cover – no, not how to eat a pizza – but taking a common-sense approach to breaking apart an inquiry and developing smaller bit-sized chunks to support students engaging in and accessing the learning.

In Chapter 2, we explored concepts at a macro level; our attention turns again to conceptual understanding.

This chapter will cover:

- **Questions, questions everywhere and not all need answering**
- **Defining concepts**
- **Concepts to frame learning**

- Inquiries within an inquiry (mini inquiries)
- Order in the inquiry
- The sum of the parts
- Auditing the concepts across the year
- Don't leave them on the planner

Questions, questions everywhere and not all need answering

Let's use the understanding from chapter 4: 'Natural disasters disrupt lives and livelihoods'. When I see a statement like this, I really hope my students will look at this and ask lots of questions. The task for teachers is to do the same, not necessarily in an attempt to pre-empt student questions, but to pull it apart and see what it actually means.

The more you can ask questions as a collaborative teaching group, the stronger the questioning and the depth of collective understanding. Looking at that statement, these are the questions that spring to mind (and by spring, some do and others take a while longer):

- How do natural disasters disrupt lives and livelihoods?
- Do all natural disasters disrupt lives and livelihoods?
- What are natural disasters?
- Is it only natural disasters that disrupt lives and livelihoods?
- What other types of disasters are there?
- What is the difference between lives and livelihoods?
- What does disrupt mean?
- How disruptive are natural disasters?
- Are all lives and livelihoods disrupted by natural disasters?
- Where in the world do these natural disasters take place?
- Why do natural disasters disrupt lives and livelihoods?
- Can we prevent natural disasters?
- Can we protect against natural disasters?
- Are humans directly impacting natural disasters?
- Does where people live determine how they are impacted by natural disasters?

Going back over those questions there are two things I would bear in mind. The first is: 'Do I think that all of these are answerable through the scope of the inquiry I am setting up?' and the second is: 'What concepts are they each exploring?'

Some may fall in the scope of learning, others without. Never discard a question, always honour your thinking behind it, but... they may not be driving forces behind your inquiry. Your students will ask more questions (hopefully) and not all of theirs will be answered by you – although you could provide the time and space for them!

Defining concepts

A great strategy to develop an understanding of what a concept is (by definition) is to engage in an activity called 'Take a Stand'. Take a Stand is a simple strategy, but is powerful in its ability to divine thinking and elicit an understanding or shared view of something. The strategy is a decision-making approach that encourages individuals to take a stand on an issue, rather than remain neutral or be on the fence (and you will get fence-sitters, but encourage them to make a decision). It is also physical and involves movement, so it gets participants off their seats and engaged in an activity fully. As you are going to get them to think, they are also engaging cognitive processes.

The ideal is that you don't actually teach at all – it is beautifully inquiry bound, where those participating explore after stimulus and come up with their own collective working definitions. You provide the time and the space, along with the stimulus. Be mindful also that you may have to ask some probing questions to ensure that there is depth and rigour to their thinking. Another factor to consider is that when you hear something that is worth recording as part of the working definition, ask questions like 'Did you want me to write that down as part of our definition?' or 'Does anyone agree or disagree with that before we write that down? or 'Does your thinking fit with our working definition?'

When introducing it, establish the ground rules:

1. You must make a decision to stand on either side of the room – the middle is not an option.
2. Once you've decided, you must be prepared to justify your decision.
3. Anyone could be called upon.

4. After listening to others' reasoning, you are able to change where you stand.
5. Through this, you will come up with a definition of what a concept is.

When doing this with groups of teachers, I always place a few little caveats around rule number 2. Specifically, they are in regard to non-participation or getting away without having a good answer. Each of these can only be used once by the group, so if they are said early by someone, then no one else can use it:

- I chose this side because my friends are there.
- I chose this side because most people went there.
- I chose this side because _____ is smart and I went wherever they went.

The two polar opposites that staff can decide to align or stand with are 'Content' or 'Concept'. You need to have prepared some words (just single words) that will fall under either heading. The following is the list of words that I have used on occasion. The words are not a recommendation, purely suggestions:

Content	Concept
Chocolate	Friendship
Grass	Sorrow
Pencil	Patience
Patients	Love
Surfboard	Equity

You only need to explore as many as is required until you have a working definition and can test and prove it. Going through the list because you have made it is an exercise in providing opportunities for people to become bored and disengage. You may get some very lateral thinkers who take it upon themselves to prove their cognitive muscles and argue that something that is unanimously agreed upon (except themselves) and fits the definition of concepts is the opposite (or vice versa). If you encounter this, draw back to the strength of the definition, honour and acknowledge their thinking and seek the reinforcement of the other position from the other side of the room.

Allowing the participants to come up with their own definition is a brave exercise as it is potentially risky. However, if you choose your words carefully and identify those moments to press more and clarify or seize thinking, then it will be a richly rewarding experience that will set up participants for success when understanding and ultimately working with concepts.

But you need to go in knowing where you want to end up. A working or solidified version of how you define concepts is what you need to have clearly in mind. Failing to do this could result in the direction of the conversation going off on tangents, which could then mean missing the opportunity to seize the 'gems' that come out and can support the group's understanding. My working definition that I enter into this sort of activity with is that concepts are:

- Intangible
- Timeless
- Overarching
- Transferable
- Abstract

To unpack each of these, you need to have an understanding of each of these words so that you can lead and guide staff to develop similar thinking.

- **Intangible:** Sometimes the best description is a non-example – they cannot be touched or held. At a literal level, they aren't nouns.
- **Timeless:** They can't be bound by time. A gramophone exists in a certain time. But friendship has existed and will continue to exist.
- **Overarching:** As they aren't physical, they are ideas based. But they aren't thoughts, they are umbrella ideas that smaller things fit under.
- **Transferable:** They mean different things to different people or they can be different in different settings. I love custard and I love my wife and children. But that love is different between them (the custard and my family, that is).
- **Abstract:** They aren't bound by a clear immutable definition; tying together the notions of transferable and intangible.

It does not matter if your wording is the same as above or slightly different. The important part is that you enter into this with clear a definition and understanding of what a concept means. This is so important as when someone offers "It can't be touched or held", you can capture that and offer to record it. To go a step further, you could re-cast and suggest that "Does that mean it is intangible?"

Once the definition is arrived at, test it with a few more examples and hopefully you will see that the vast majority of people move with clarity, purpose and little thought. Ideally, they just get it as they have a good definition to guide them and they can be comfortable in justifying their stance based on the definition.

With the definition of a concept developed, it is time to start exploring how they influence and impact our learning.

Concepts to frame learning

As mentioned previously, there is no definitive or finite list of concepts to explore curriculum through. When looking at concepts at this smaller level, they are very much like lenses in which to view the learning. Going for a walk on the beach, I will pop on a pair of sunglasses to help my vision, but it will also change my vision – it will make things darker. If I am at the cricket, I will get out my binoculars to help me see in better detail. When I'm driving, I need glasses to help sharpen the distance. No matter which lens I view things through, the subject I'm viewing looks different.

This is exactly what concepts do again at this level. Borrowing the understanding from chapter 4, we will explore how to find the concepts that help drive 'Natural disasters disrupt lives and livelihoods'.

Depending on the curriculum set will determine what specific content you cover. That will change how you express these, as will the age of your students. Working with our statement above, let's assume we are working with students from the Grade 3/4 part of the school.

What direction do you anticipate the learning to go? Does it need to be about how things work or why things occur or what they are like? The International Baccalaureate, through the Primary Years Program, identified in concepts that they believe extend through all learning. Their list is: change, connection, causation, form, function, responsibility and perspective.

This list of concepts is strong and based on evidence, and they work! Using these or a list of your own choosing will definitely help guide, support and inform how to break down the inquiry further.

Using the list of concepts to categorise our questions from earlier, it is a quick audit following from a little understanding of what the concepts mean.

- **Change** – Explores what is changing or how it has changed.
- **Connection** – Explores the possible connections between one thing and another.
- **Causation** – Explores the causes or reasons for something occurring. It really asks the question why.
- **Form** – Explores what something is like at a physical level.
- **Function** – Explores how things work.
- **Responsibility** – Explores what is the responsibility we have in relation to something.
- **Perspective** – Explores the different points of view on something.

The 'something' or 'what' in all of these is, when contextualised, replaced with your inquiry direction.

Sorting out the questions from earlier, they can be categorised into the following (note: all questions are categorised still):

Concepts	Question(s)
Change	- Does where people live determine how they are impacted by natural disasters?
Connection	-
Causation	- Why do natural disasters disrupt lives and livelihoods?
Form	- What is the difference between lives and livelihood? - What does disrupt mean? - What other types of disasters are there? - Are all lives and livelihoods disrupted by natural disasters? - What are natural disasters? - Where in the world do these natural disasters take place? - Do all natural disasters disrupt lives and livelihoods? - Is it only natural disasters that disrupt lives and livelihoods?
Function	- How do natural disasters disrupt lives and livelihoods?
Responsibility	- Can we protect against natural disasters? - Can we prevent natural disasters? - Are humans directly impacting on natural disasters?
Perspective	- How disruptive are natural disasters?

Auditing the questions that way, there are a lot of 'form' questions. That means that either form is a concept that needs exploring through this inquiry or that the questions generated are weighted towards form. I'd advocate that the questions that are most worth answering are the ones to choose, and therefore the concepts choose themselves. However, in order to broaden your students' thinking and engagement, you should choose three questions from different concepts.

In this instance, I'm choosing the following:

- How do natural disasters disrupt lives and livelihoods? (Function)
- What are natural disasters? (Form)
- Are humans directly impacting on natural disasters? (Responsibility)

Inquiries within an inquiry (mini inquiries)

With those three questions and concepts identified, we need to go deeper and within. When *Inception* first hit our movie screens in 2010, heads were spinning from the layers within layers within layers, within layers, etc. Our heads won't hurt as much understanding the following logic as all we are doing is breaking up the inquiry into smaller parts. The suggested number of 'chunks' to break up an inquiry into is three, as each of these will become their own separate inquiry. The idea behind this is that the statement is broken apart into more digestible pieces (slices of pizza).

Cases can be made for two or four on some occasions, but they are rare and come with their own shortcomings. Going with two doesn't seem to break apart the statement far enough or broadly enough. The case against four is that you may not have enough time to explore and engage with each of them sufficiently. Some inquiries, depending on how you map and allocate them, can be as short as five or six weeks, which doesn't allow for the necessary depth of discovery if there are too many foci.

I like to start these with a sentence starter, such as: 'We are inquiring into…' Then the thinking and statements developed need to fit into this to complete a sentence to make the mini inquiries.

Taking our questions from above, we can almost drop them in as our mini inquiries.

We are inquiring into…

- How do natural disasters disrupt lives and livelihoods? (Function)

- What are natural disasters? (Form)
- Are humans directly impacting on natural disasters? (Responsibility)

With a little revision and playing with our structures, we can quickly turn them into:

We are inquiring into…
- How natural disasters disrupt lives and livelihoods (Function)
- Natural disasters (Form)
- Human impact on natural disasters (Responsibility)

As again, presenting the students with statements rather than questions is highly preferable.

Order in the inquiry

Don't picture a judge coming down with a gavel and demanding order. Looking at the above mini inquiries, there is a case to be made that they are not in a logical sequence. In the case above, it seems illogical to explore the why of natural disaster before students know what natural disasters are. I would shuffle the order around to ensure that the order of these is logical and developmental.

We are inquiring into:
- Natural disasters (Form)
- How natural disasters disrupt lives and livelihoods (Function)
- Human impact on natural disasters (Responsibility)

The sum of the parts

Creating your mini inquiries within the inquiry serves a simple purpose: to break down the main understanding. There is nothing to be gained from going off on tangents and exploring ideas and going down conversational rabbit holes. Someone in the group (or from outside the group) needs to keep the conversation and thinking on the right track. You will have numerous accountabilities that need to be considered, such as:

- Curriculum mapped
- Previous learning experiences
- The timing in the year

- Student learning needs
- Conceptual considerations
- Age appropriateness
- Sticking to your statement/understanding

Stepping back and auditing in the middle of the process can save angst and anguish (and time) were you to leave the reflection until the end. Always keep the statement firmly in your mind and know where your inquiry has to go. I know there are people who will argue (and rightfully so) that the students should determine where the learning goes. The challenge faced in many schools is 'How do I do that while ensuring that I cover curriculum?'

My intention in directing staff to be conscious of where their inquiry has to go is to ensure that they are honouring their curriculum accountabilities – as many schools and governing or regulatory bodies make this absolutely compulsory. Curriculum can be a minimum, though. If we cover the areas we need to and then allow the students to explore the areas they would like to, then we can do both! Gone are the days of the sage on the stage. It is time to be the guide on the side.

Auditing the concepts across the year

After completing this process for all the inquiries across the year, the next thing to do is to audit the distribution of concepts across the year. No fancy tool or mechanism is needed here, just observation and tallying.

Review all the inquiries and their concepts. A balanced year of conceptual learning will include a reasonably equally distributed allocation of concepts. If you have seven concepts and six inquiries, then you have the capacity to distribute seven concepts across 18 possible statements. It can't be even, so try to seek what is reasonable when auditing.

If you had something like the following, I think you would have cause for some serious review:

Change	Connection	Causation	Form	Function	Responsibility	Perspective
IIII	IIII	IIII	IIII		II	

A balanced program of learning would ensure that there was a more evenly distributed coverage of concepts. The above table indicates that the students would not have explicit coverage of the concepts of Function and Perspective. They would be well placed to cover and have a deeper working knowledge of Change, Connection, Causation and Form. But those come at the expense of others.

If your allocation looks like this at the end of when you have allocated your concepts, then you need to go back and review to see how you could redistribute them. It will also call for a change of thinking and wording of your mini inquiries that stem from them. It simply can't be a rewording as the essence of what you are exploring is different. Therefore, the thinking needs to start anew and in essence start from scratch.

One way to avoid this is to keep a tally of the concepts as you align them to your inquiries (and development of mini inquiries). This will save the potential rethinking and reworking after completing the whole year. Have someone in the group allocated to record these as you progress and be 'that voice' that keeps you thinking about the variation and coverage across the year.

Change	Connection	Causation	Form	Function	Responsibility	Perspective
III	II	III	II	III	III	II

Ideally, the above table would look like what you want to aim for. There is a reasonable spread of concepts across the year and while it is not even, it is reasonably equitable. The task now is to review and observe what the spread looks like over the entire school. Teams will have developed their own, potentially seven across the primary school, which would mean that there are potentially 126 concepts that can be distributed.

If each team were to produce the same distribution for Form and Function, which while highly unlikely, it is a possibility. If it was the case, then Form would only be covered 14 times across the school year by students. And the other side of that equation is that Function would be covered on 21 occasions. This equates to 50% more coverage, which seems pretty unfair. When viewed from this position, it creates quite a disparity in the concepts explored. It may well be the case that you are hoping to cover Function more than Form – that achieves that. However, it is important to provide a variety of concepts to ensure that all are understood and experienced by students fairly.

A way to view this is to audit at the end of all teams completing their concept allocations, but that means that energy has potentially been spent and ideas in the form of mini inquiries would have to get changed. To guard against this, have someone who is floating (potentially someone from leadership or not allocated to a classroom) and have them conduct an ongoing audit as teams develop them. Their role won't be to create and allocate concepts but to point out what they are observing across the school and potentially steer teams to consider which concepts may need more explicit coverage. Another strategy is to have the audit digitally where it can be seen by anyone and changes are reflected in real time.

Don't leave them on the planner

With all the hard work, thinking and preplanning to establish the inquiry, concepts and mini inquiries, pop them onto the planner or overview before they are lost. But that is not where it finishes. Don't leave them on the planner and become part of the conversation that teachers have and never explicitly and directly discuss these with the students. Display them, talk about them, show your tally of coverage over the year. Don't let this be the realm of teachers – draw back the curtain and expose the Wizard of Oz working feverishly in the background.

It isn't that scary, it isn't overawing, it isn't too hard for the students.

- Work with your students to help them understand what concepts are (Form).
- Make them aware of how concepts work (Function).
- Discuss how concepts may look different depending on content or experience (Perspective).
- Educate the students as to why concepts are important in their learning (Causation).
- Explore how concepts change the way content can be viewed (Change).
- Find ways to seek links between concepts or between how concepts have been covered or explored in different areas of their learning (Connection).
- Challenge them to see it as a shared responsibility to understand and use these in the learning (Responsibility).

Chapter summary

- Explore questions when unpacking your inquiry.
- Write as many as you can and audit them against a conceptual framework in order to view the types of questions being asked.
- Define a conceptual framework in which you are operating at an inquiry level (not a macro one).
- Using concepts to frame the learning enhances the capacity to build onto previous learning.
- Audit how concepts are explicitly aligned and taught across the year.
- Make sure you ask the questions or provide space for students to ask questions; don't just leave them on the planner.

Reflection

A great way to have people explore a topic/concept is through the thinking routine called Chalk Talk designed through Harvard's Project Zero. Chalk Talk is a thinking routine designed to allow participants to contribute, silently, to a number of stimuli. The collective thinking of the room is built through each person's participation and contributions.

Things to do beforehand to be organised:

- Divide people into even groups.
- Have enough markers for each person.
- Have your statements/images on large paper and allocate them across the space.

Basic rules:

- No verbal communication is allowed.
- People are to move from one statement to the other in one of two ways: free roaming or timed, it is your choice.
- Participants can:
    - Record by writing a response to the statement or an other's statement.
    - Ask or answer a question.
    - Link previously recorded items.
    - Use symbols such as a tick (check mark), cross or question mark to responses.

On large sheets of paper, place statements that will generate responses from your staff on the topic of concept-based learning. They can be truths, assumptions, challenges, untruths or purely provocative statements. The greater the range, the more 'conversation' you will get from the activity.

Begin the protocol and roam the room, observing and contributing, if you wish.

Below is a list of statements you could use…

- Concept-based learning does not alone guarantee a deeper understanding of a subject.
- Concept-based learning enables students to gain a deeper understanding of a subject by connecting concepts to one another.
- Concepts are an essential part of the education process.
- Concepts do not need to be explicitly shared with the students.
- Concept-based learning is not a panacea for all educational ills.
- Concept-based learning should not be seen as a replacement for more traditional forms of teaching.
- Concept-based learning helps develop a student's problem-solving skills.
- Concepts are confusing to students.
- If we want to encourage cognitive dissonance, then concepts are essential.
- Concepts help students link abstract and previously disconnected ideas.

For a more in-depth description of Chalk Talk, visit www.pz.harvard.edu/sites/default/files/Chalk%20Talk_1.pdf

CHAPTER 7

MAPPING THE YEAR

"Australia will not close the ever-widening achievement gap between disadvantaged and advantaged students unless we solve the curriculum planning problems in our schools"
– **Grattan Institute (2022)**

"All mixed up in the wash. Hot bleeding our colours"
– **Cold War Kids: 'Hang Me Up to Dry'**

In the early stages of my career, I was presented with the problem of 'just in time' teaching or 'just in case' teaching. It struck me that just in time learning made the most sense, because it has the immediacy of application and the capacity to readily apply the new learning. As I progressed in my career, there were justifiable opportunities for 'just in case' teaching, but those came infrequently. Upon learning about the *cognitive load theory*, my thinking changed almost straight away.

We have all had moments when there is just so much information coming at us or we have a to-do list that is ludicrous in its length that we can feel that tension rise (giving rise to fight or flight), and the ability to process or take on anything further is too much. This is not a positive way to be for any period of time, even briefly. We cannot process any new information. Imagine being in a classroom with a basic understanding of numbers. You can count forwards, backwards, skip count, even identify a half. Then your teacher says that in this lesson you are going to learn about quarters, eighths, thirds, sixths and compare them in size. For some students that may be achievable. For some it will be beyond a struggle. But if you spent five minutes teaching one and quickly move on to the next, and then the next, etc, there would not be a significant amount of retention!

Cognitive load theory is like a buffet – it helps us decide which items we should take in order to maximise the benefit and minimise the cost. Just like a buffet, there is a limit to the amount that can be taken in at one time, and it is important to prioritise the most important items and leave the rest. If we overload the plate, we risk not being able to digest all the information properly. Similarly, if we overload our brains with too much information, we risk not being able to process it all and use it effectively. At some point we all reach a capacity; knowing the capacity of your class, and individual learners within the class, is paramount.

"Cognitive load theory is an instructional theory based on our knowledge of human cognition" (Sweller, Ayres & Kalyuga, 2011). In essence, cognitive load theory suggests that the human brain has a specific capacity for taking in new information at one time. It also suggests that there is a limit to what we can process at a given moment and advocates for smaller building blocks of information, allowing new information in smaller chunks. This in turn allows our working memory to integrate this new information into existing systems of memory.

The question then is: "Does just in time teaching reinforce the notion of loading up too much?" The answer isn't simply black and white – there are shades of grey in here. It all depends on the timing and how you map out the year.

In any academic year, there will always be school holidays, camps, closures, public holidays, internal events, religious and/or secular festivals or commemorations. We know that the time we have (approximately 40 weeks of instructional time) is impacted by factors beyond the control of the classroom teacher or even school leadership/administration. If these dates are known, then it makes sense to plan around them – which is what most schools do. But that is only part of the equation.

Planning the year, as seen in Chapter 3, has planned the inquiries for the year. At this point you know what is being covered, but not necessarily when. If there are five inquiries you have planned for a particular level or grades, then you have on average eight weeks per inquiry. Some may be longer; while some may be shorter, as outlined in Chapter 3. But the sequence now is key.

This chapter will explore the following topics:
- **Articulating the year**
- **Recording how the inquiries are sequenced**

- Displaying the inquiries
- Sequencing the curriculum
- Aligning the curriculum
- Documenting the inquiry
- Involvement is key
- How to create GANTT charts with Excel

Articulating the year

Either on a whiteboard or on pieces of paper (or digitally if that works for you), plot all the known dates for the upcoming year. There will be some periods of time when certain levels are impacted by events more than others, but as a leadership team, create a template. In Australia, the National Assessment Program – Literacy and Numeracy (NAPLAN) is a centralised testing period for Literacy and Numeracy that occurs in March for students in Grades 3, 5, 7 and 9. There is little to no impact on students in other year levels, therefore, it shouldn't be a factor for them in their planning. This is a common practice to plan for these in this way, but let's get a little more micro.

Example template

	Date	#	Public Holidays	School Closures	School Events	Camps	Pre-Booked Excursions	Religious Events	Emergency Drills	External Sporting	Photo Days	Parent Evenings	Board Meetings	Learning Conferences
Term 1	30-Jan	1												
	6-Feb	2												
	13-Feb	3												
	20-Feb	4												
	27-Feb	5												
	6-Mar	6												
	13-Mar	7												
	20-Mar	8												
	27-Mar	9												
	3-Apr	10												
Term 2	24-Apr	1												
	1-May	2												
	8-May	3												
	15-May	4												
	22-May	5												
	29-May	6												
	5-Jun	7												
	12-Jun	8												
	19-Jun	9												
	10-Jul	1												

By completing a template like the above, you get a sense of when the key events are on over the course of the year. If there is a camp planned for a year level that incorporates a certain content area, then that is when the learning should be aligned. What is required then is the thinking to determine when in that inquiry the camp best fits. Is it at the beginning, the middle, the end? The items on the top of the page are flexible and should be changed to suit your context. Consider prioritising them from left to right in order of importance or levels of flexibility.

Once a year is fully articulated with the dates identified, schools are then in a position to identify which of the inquiries fits best within the context of the school setting and calendar. And adjusting for length allows you to ensure that inquiries start and finish in alignment with school-based calendars and balanced against the planned duration of inquiries.

The more organised teachers (or most people) feel, the more confident and willing they are to take risks or to explore new and different things. By liberating the macro-planning for the year, and some meso-planning, it allows teachers to focus on the micro (the day-to-day; lesson) planning, which is the instructional key to learning. But we are not yet ready to refine that far just yet.

Recording how the inquiries are sequenced

Depending on whether you have individual grades or two or more grades, experiencing the same inquiry is a localised decision. The example below illustrates how inquiries can be sequenced over the course of a year. Colour is a far greater way to differentiate the different inquiry foci than this shaded and italicised example:

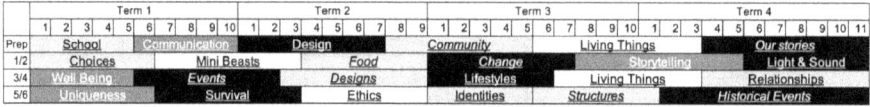

With all the decisions made, there is something to reflect on at this point and acknowledge the efforts that have been undertaken to reach this point. Each of the 'summaries' of the inquiries is identified and hyperlinked to the planners for each inquiry. This makes this file (if you create it digitally) a quick reference point for all staff in your school to identify what is occurring in different settings, but also a quick way to access all the planners, without having to dive through the school's digital filing system.

With the sequence of learning set, it is now paramount to map the other, up to this point intentionally ignored, curricula. For just about every school, these are the two big ones: Literacy and Mathematics. Depending on what curriculum you follow/offer, it may be the case that Religious Education, wellbeing, meditation, mindfulness, specialist subject areas or other areas need to be mapped.

Displaying the inquiries

To support the digital version, displaying a colourful and public large version of this is also advisable. The power of being so transparent with the learning across the school means that every single learner, staff member and visitor to the school can see what learning is being focused on over the course of the year and at that moment in time. This provides a quick insight as to what is occurring across the school without providing too much detail and overwhelming the viewer.

Placing it centrally and publicly is the important part – it need not be a glamorous setting or prime real estate in the school foyer. As seen in the example below (with my less than fantastic handwriting, it can be on cupboard doors in a walkway).

Example of inquiries display

Sequencing the curriculum

If you've ever experienced the stress-free and glorious process that is building a house, then I'm pretty certain you're viewing it with rose-coloured glasses (see what lenses do!). Building a house – or any other structure – can be a long process involving many individuals and requires energy, resources and planning. In order to plan out time, people and timings, GANTT charts are used.

GANTT charts are a highly effective way of mapping out a schedule or project. So, why don't we use them or something similar?

GANTT charts can be used in sequencing learning in schools incorporating cognitive load theory by helping teachers to sequence learning that is within their students' cognitive load capacity. By breaking larger tasks into smaller, more manageable chunks, teachers can help ensure that their students are not overwhelmed by the task. GANTT charts can be used in sequencing learning in schools by providing a visual representation of the activities and tasks that need to be completed in order to reach a desired outcome – in this case, sequencing learning to scaffold and build knowledge.

With an overly simplified interpretation of potential learning, there are three versions of how to sequence learning, using Mathematics, Literacy and Science as curriculum examples: just in case learning vs just in time learning (traditional) vs flow of learning.

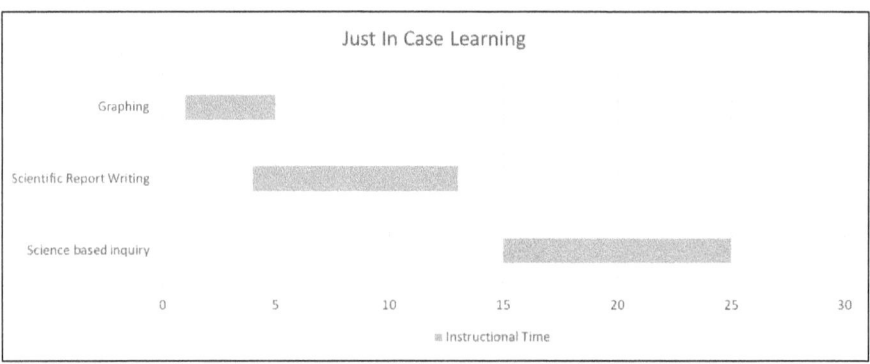

Just in case learning outlines that learning happens in isolation bearing no relationship to other learning. This is very much teaching in silos, where each piece of information is sorted separately and demands a significant amount of supposition on behalf of the learner to join disconnected knowledge and skills without application. In light of cognitive load theory, this may appear to be quite in alignment with that approach. However, this would only be accurate in a world where only one subject or curriculum area was taught at a time for a period of weeks.

In reality, the students would be learning something in Literacy, something in Mathematics and their science-based inquiry. This more than makes the case for just in time learning or a flow of learning.

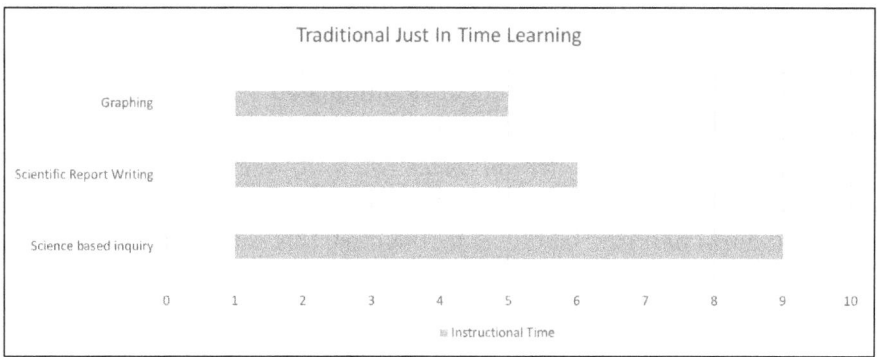

Now this makes more sense! If I am teaching (or the students are experiencing/learning) through a science-based inquiry, then there are opportunities to connect and teach the Literacy and Mathematics skills and content that link and support the inquiry. This is traditionally how integrated or inquiry-based learning merges curriculum to address the competing interests.

Considered through the lens of cognitive load theory, what we are demanding of the learners in this model is: learn new information about Literacy and Mathematics and apply it to a science-based inquiry they are currently learning. Everything they are learning or experiencing is new – that is beyond what cognitive load theorists would advocate for. But it is significantly better, as there are at least connections and conceptual links that can be made through them all. It is still a lot of new learning all at once.

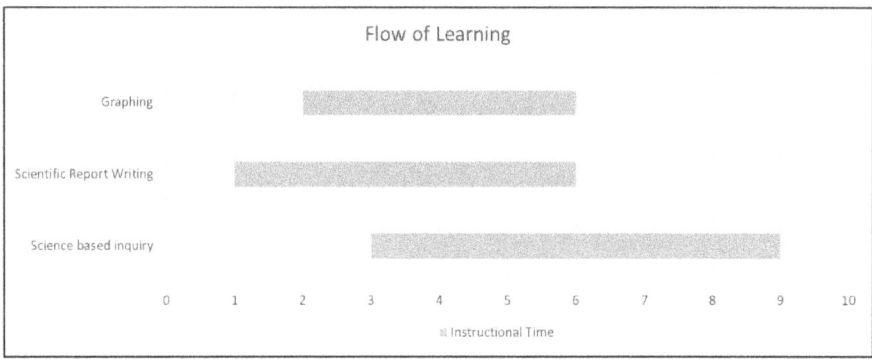

The above demonstrates a 'flow of learning' that shifts the balance of learning 'new' content and skills to ensure the students have them ready to apply rather than learn them all synchronously. Working with the knowledge that the previous inquiry is in its later phases and there are degrees of independence in the learning rather than explicit instructional teaching, Literacy and Mathematics are manipulated to ensure the cognitive load is shared. They commence learning about scientific report writing just ahead of time. This model demonstrates two solid weeks of learning about scientific report writing that the students have ready to apply. As graphs and tables can form part of scientific report writing, this can be introduced just prior to application as well.

The timing of these elements is illustrative only, and as a teacher, you know how long your students would need for each to ensure the flow of learning is appropriate and timely.

Aligning the curriculum

It now becomes an important part of planning to merge all the ideas and have a singular document that outlines the foci and timespan for all the learning that is planned to occur over the course of the academic year.

As seen in the previous table, there is a cadence or flow of learning. The inquiry that focuses on creativity lends itself to supporting poetry as the text to explore with students (or poetry lends itself to supporting the inquiry). Instead of starting poetry at the same time as the inquiry on creativity, it is brought forward by two weeks so the students can access the skills early and apply them in the inquiry, rather than learning both at the same time. This is a supportive way to lighten the cognitive load on students and allow them to have transference of knowledge.

Sensibly, the table opposite shows that there is a school concert coming up. The poetry may or may not fit in with the performance, but if it did, doesn't it make sense to do all the learning before the production rather than at the same time when it could be too late? It may even be an opportunity for the junior team to align their light and sound inquiry from the previous chapter to coincide with the concert. Nothing like the application of learnt skill!

Your eye may be drawn to the 'second' rectangle in Maths. It is intentionally blank. Not all learning has to tie in and link back to the inquiry. When we try to link everything and there isn't a genuine way to do it, we weaken both the integrity of the inquiry and the integrity of the content or subject we are attempting to integrate. So, this is when Maths may become stand-alone and not linked. Maths has a lot of content and as such, the above example provides opportunities for this content to be covered outside the inquiry.

Planning an inquiry table

Terms	One										Two									
Weeks	1	2	3	4	5	6	7	8	9	10	1	2	3	4	5	6	7	8	9	10
Inquiry	Health						Creativity							Democracy						
Literacy	Explanations					Poetry					Persuasive									
Maths	Measurement								Statistics											
School events				Open weeks			Closure day													
Specialists												PTI			Concert				Reports	
SEL																				
Other																				

Mapping the year 99

Imagine planning an inquiry and linking data to it – no problem there. The inquiry goes for nine weeks, but you don't need data to go for that long. Using the table on page 99, it allows you to demonstrate that and start and finish concepts from learning areas when they are ready to be applied. The table can be converted into a GANTT chart quite readily. Open up Sheets, Numbers or Excel and away you go!

For those so inclined to learn more, prior to the reflection section of this chapter is a 'how to' when creating GANTT charts in Excel.

The other option is to go old school and use paper and markers or even sentence strips or flashcards. Working on the theory that a flashcard has the value of one week, find a space and something to lay them down onto and map out your year. The value of physical manipulation is the ease in which you can move things around and make all the changes without having to change formulae or settings on a document.

Being physical also means that the thinking and output are visible by all and not inhibited by one person on a screen. Even if someone is displaying it on a larger projection, there is really only one person who can drive it and maintain the changes. Making it physical allows for anyone in the team to be active in the manipulation and placement of items. It also means that anyone walking in (leaders, single-subject teacher/specialist or other) can at a moment's glance see exactly what is happening. The same can be said for a computer using a projector, but at some point, it will be unclear due to formatting, changing or input at a data level (rather than a graph).

Documenting the inquiry

Once you've 'finished' your curriculum mapping, where is it documented? There have been a few options offered to display and document the curriculum; some show the timings, the sequence and the starting and ending points (the dynamism). Another alternative is to document the whole mapped curriculum in a linear way. I am not advocating for work in triplication here, simply that this is an alternate way to document the mapped curriculum once it is aligned to inquiries.

There are two distinct ways in which to document linearly. The first is by sequencing macro concept and the other by sequence.

By macro concept

As can be seen in the table below, the learning is sequenced by macro concept. With all the inquiries and macro concepts colour coded (or grey-scaled here), each and every year level will be articulated in the same order. If you want to view the learning for a particular macro concept, you know it will be first on every page. You just need space to indicate that it is the first or third, etc.

A consideration to have is as it reads by concept, not by order of teaching, it may take some adjusting.

Learning sequenced by macro concept table

	Unit 2 – 6 weeks T1W7 – T2W3	Unit 5 – 6 weeks T3W7 – T4W2	Unit 4 – 6 weeks T3W1 – T3W6	Unit 3 – 7 weeks T2W3 – T2W10	Unit 1 – 6 weeks T1W1 – T1W6	Unit 6 – 6 weeks T4W3 – T4W8
	Concept 1	Concept 2	Concept 3	Concept 4	Concept 5	Concept 6
	Definitions/ explanations/ scope of learning	Definitions/ explanations/ scope of learning	Definitions/ explanations/ scope of learning	Definitions/ explanations/ scope of learning	Definitions/ explanations/ scope of learning	Definitions/ explanations/ scope of learning
	Understanding					
	I change as I grow	Some things change over time	We connect through cultural experiences	Living things have basic needs	My behaviour impacts relationships	Different resources create light and sound
1	*Key Concepts*					
	•	•	•	•	•	•
	We are inquiring into...					
	Skills addressed					
	•	•	•	•	•	•
	Links to English					
	•	•	•	•	•	•
	Links to Mathematics					
	•	•	•	•	•	•
	Links to Social and Emotional Learning					
	•	•	•	•	•	•
	Curriculum Links (reportable areas in italics and red)					
	•	•	•	•	•	•
	Possible excursions / incursions					
	•	•	•	•	•	•
	Other					

By sequence

As this subheading suggests, the inquiries and aligned curriculum are documented in the order they will be experienced by the students. As shown in the table below, there is a clear left to right order of the inquiries. None of the learning has changed from the version above, just the sequence honoured.

A consideration, if documenting in this manner, is that it is sequenced by time, not macro concept. When reviewing the year, looking for colour will be the easiest way to search by macro concept. If it is colour coded well, then you just look for a colour and tune your brain to look for that colour.

Learning sequenced by macro concept table – with the sequence honoured

	Unit 1 – 5 weeks T1W1 – T1W5	Unit 2 – 6 weeks T1W7 – T2W2	Unit 3 – 7 weeks T2W3 – T2W10	Unit 4 – 6 weeks T3W1 – T3W6	Unit 5 – 6 weeks T3W7 – T4W2	Unit 6 – 6 weeks T4W3 – T4W8
	Concept 5	**Concept 1**	**Concept 4**	**Concept 3**	**Concept 2**	**Concept 6**
	Definitions/ explanations/ scope of learning	Definitions/ explanations/ scope of learning	Definitions/ explanations/ scope of learning	Definitions/ explanations/ scope of learning	Definitions/ explanations/ scope of learning	Definitions/ explanations/ scope of learning
		**Understanding**				
1	• My behaviour impacts relationships	• I change as I grow	Living things have basic needs	We connect through cultural experiences	Some things change over time	Different resources create light and sound
		**Key Concepts**				
		**We are inquiring into...**				
		**Skills addressed**				
	•	•	•	•	•	•
		**Links to English**				
	•	•	•	•	•	•
		**Links to Mathematics**				
	•	•	•	•	•	•
		**Links to Social and Emotional Learning**				
	•	•	•	•	•	•
		**Curriculum Links** *(reportable areas in italics and red)*				
	•	•	•	•	•	•
		**Possible excursions / incursions**				
	•	•	•	•	•	•
		**Other**				

Does the order matter on this document?

Not at all. It only matters that your school does them in the same way in each team. You can't have some ordering by sequence and some by macro concept. There needs to be an approach taken by the school and agreed upon if this is the way you choose to document your mapped curriculum.

Involvement is key

The key behind the entire process is the capacity to have multiple people's perspectives and inputs throughout the process. Again, this comes down to ownership and understanding. The more of that you can build into any curriculum, the greater the possible end point, which leads to empowered teachers knowing what they are teaching and they are motivated and energised to present it to and engage students in it.

Imagine that feeling that staff have of not having to worry or utilise their hard-earned holidays with that dreaded question 'What will I teach or when will I teach it?' Mapping out your curriculum in the school year prior means summer holidays can be enjoyed for their purpose. Mapping a school's curriculum for the year doesn't solve all the curriculum issues that schools face, but going through the process does allay a significant number of fears and anxieties.

Mapping the curriculum doesn't, however, cover the 'how' of teaching. This is very much dependent on your school's pedagogical approach. If your school is one of constructivism, then you now get to contemplate how you will teach that content through the constructivist approach. Or the 'how' can be how do we engage our students in the learning through the activities we plan for them. The 'how' can even extend to how do we assess student learning in our inquiries.

How to create GANTT charts with Excel

Step 1. Enter the content or learning areas in column A (starting in Row 2).

Step 2. In Rows C and D, provide the headings Starting Week and Instructional Time respectively. Then enter the relevant starting weeks and duration. It should look like this:

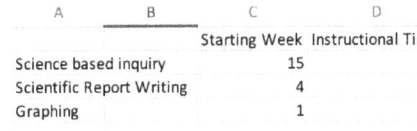

Step 3. Highlight all the data, then click on 'Insert', mouse down to chart, and then select 'Bar':

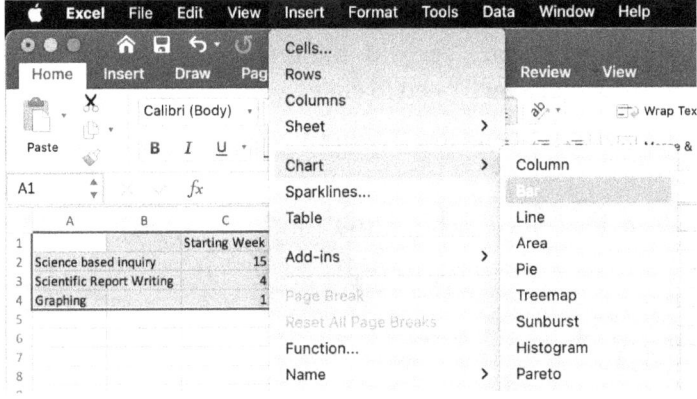

It will come out like a standard bar chart, and now we have to change it to look like a GANTT chart. But we only want to show one set of data.

Step 4. Double-click on the data on the left of the bar graph:

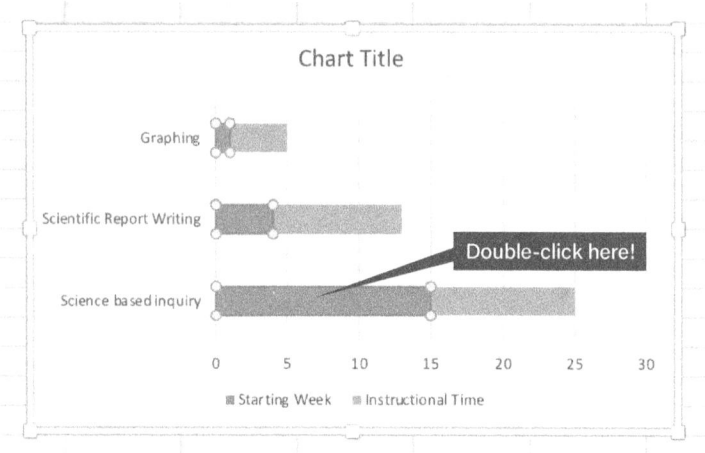

After double-clicking (you'll see with the section highlighted with the little circles in the corners), you'll need to change the colour.

The ability to change the colour should pop up on the right-hand side of the sheet.

All you need to do now is click on 'No fill' (under the tipped paint bucket tab):

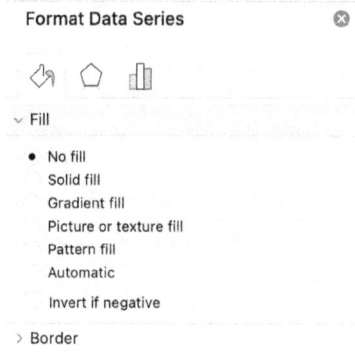

Step 5. To change the title from the generic, simply double-click on the title and call it what is most appropriate for you.

Step 6. You'll notice that there are two series on the bottom of the graph:
- Starting Week
- Instructional Time

Click on 'Starting Week' once – that will highlight them both. Next, double-click on 'Starting Week'. It should bring up the below screen:

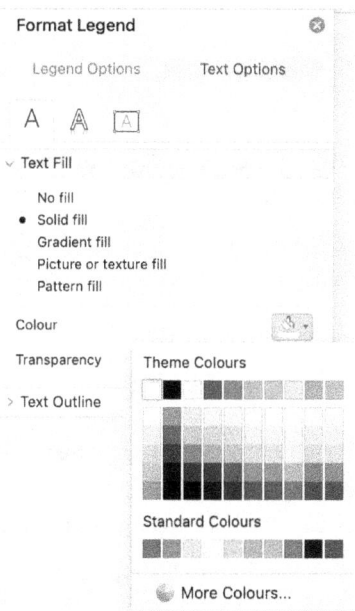

Select 'Text Outline', then the fill bucket and change the font colour to white (essentially making the text disappear!).

Chapter summary

- Mapping out the year in terms of length and sequence of inquiry is paramount.
- Establish how you will map the other elements of the curriculum or school calendar.
- Align the curriculum so it is articulated for all to view.
- Provide the opportunity for transparency and collaboration – people working in isolation will not benefit from the vision and knowledge of others.

- Document the inquiry and the related learning on a singular document that is a functional and working document.
- Ensure that as many members of staff have the opportunity to contribute to the understanding and construction of the alignment and articulation of intended learning.
- Use the quick guide of how to make a GANTT chart using technology.

Reflection

Mapping a year is a big task; take some time to reflect on your current reality by contemplating the following questions:

- How do you align your curriculum?
- Do Literacy and Maths align when your inquiries begin? Why/why not?
- At what time of year do you align all your curriculum?
- What are the non-negotiables in your school that have to be planned around?
- If you are a faith-based school, are there any festivals, special days or events that determine the dates or the length of your inquiries? Do these come first and then others are planned around them? Or vice versa?
- Who is involved in the curriculum mapping? Is this the task of leaders/coordinators/teams/everyone?
- Where do you document this mapping once it is completed? And who gets to see it?

CHAPTER 8

ASSESSING THE LEARNING

"Assessment is today's means of modifying tomorrow's instruction"
– Carol Ann Tomlinson (2000)

"The horizon begins to fade, fade, fade, fade away"
– Jack Johnson: 'The Horizon Has Been Defeated'

How many times have you found yourself just about to finish off your unit and you ask: how am I going to assess the learning? Or what exactly am I assessing? Or, even worse, how do I make judgement calls against student progress? All these questions are unfortunately all too common and normal and appear in many schools, however, they don't need to be!

Initially, as a classroom teacher, I always found the challenge of assessment to be far greater than any other facet of the role. I'd rather plan a week, deal with a challenging parent or do a double yard duty. I always found it challenging to assess the learning – particularly that of an inquiry. No problem with Literacy or Mathematics – we had books, templates, anecdotal notebooks, expectations as well. But inquiries tended to be a bit looser and there was no direction or clarity around how or what we had to assess. We knew what we were assessing (most of the time!), but lacked the ability to have consensus on what constituted certain marks.

Rubrics are now extremely commonplace in the teaching domain. But the questions that surround them that matter are the focus of this chapter, and include:

- Who makes them and how do you create them?
- Who understands them?
- How do you assess those at the polar ends of the scale?
- Who assesses against them?

- When do you create them?
- Which direction do you go?

Who makes them and how do you create them?

The simple and worst possible answer is to jump online and search for one. Please don't fall into this trap of mass-produced, fast-food-styled learning. You scramble to understand and find one that goes close to what you want, or you just accept one as 'near enough'. The parents in your school community (hopefully 100% of them) don't want 'near enough' for their child/children. Home schooling is an option for many, but these parents have made an active choice to send their child to your school and want the best from you for their child.

By investing in the process of development you are investing in the understanding, ownership and capacity to follow the rubric. The massive bonus is that each participant in the process is a part of the development and can see how their thinking (probably even direct words) are displayed in the final product. They have a real sense of 'I made that' and that cannot be gained in any other manner other than actively participating in the creation.

There are many incarnations of a rubric; the one outlined in this chapter is that of having an 'expected level' with a column either side either demonstrating above the standard or working toward the standard. While I have used rubrics where points are allocated and total to a final score, they have boundaries and sharp edges. There is no scope for demonstration of skills beyond that of the highest level. And while the previous paragraph seems to contradict this ideology, there is possibility to extend beyond the simple three-column approach.

Having been introduced to the world of rubrics at the beginning of my teaching career (particularly for Literacy), it served me well in establishing criteria for success. We would often create these with the students and ensure that there was a sense of ownership. I was fortunate enough to encounter Lane Clarke and be entirely confronted and overwhelmed by the energy and cognitive challenge provided. Of the many incredible takeaways, one was the process called Think it Great™. This was a process to determine either essential criteria or the basis of a rubric.

To outline the process, I'll use the idea of an orange. I'm not sure if this would ever be used in the classroom, but it works for illustrative purposes!

Step 1. With a flashcard provided to both participants (each having their own flashcard), they are asked to write down all the things that we believe makes an orange:

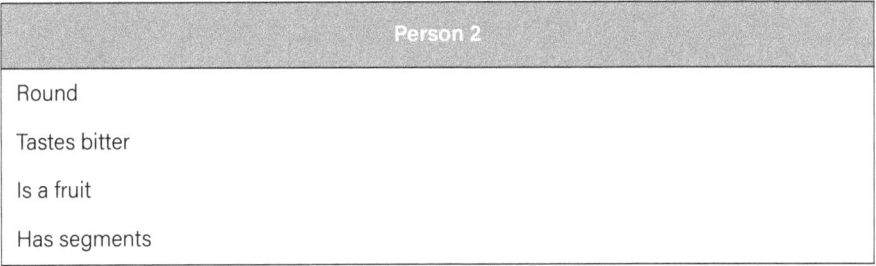

Person 1
Fruit
Orange
It has pips
It tastes sweet
Round

Person 2
Round
Tastes bitter
Is a fruit
Has segments

Step 2. It is time to compare the two and see what we have in common and what is different. The best way is to provide a fresh flashcard for the two to use together. A trusty Venn diagram is a great way to compare the two sets of ideas:

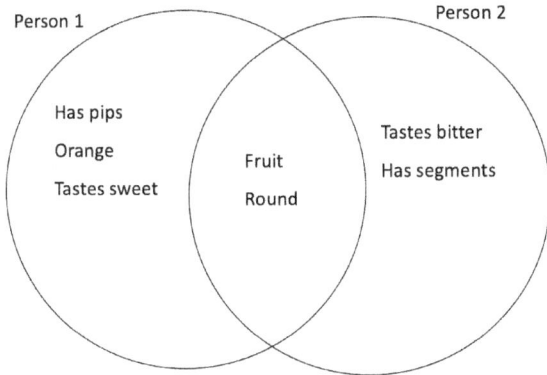

Assessing the learning   109

Step 3. With the two items in the middle of the Venn diagram, we can safely assume that these are what we will move forward with as a pair. But what of the elements on the outside areas of the Venn diagram? What can we do with them to see whether they should be included or excluded? Test them.

The simplest way to test them is to read out and either cross off those you don't agree on or place ticks or crosses next to all the items. Once you've gone through all the items, you now have a list of criteria you both agree on that constitutes an orange. It is worth recording this as seen below...

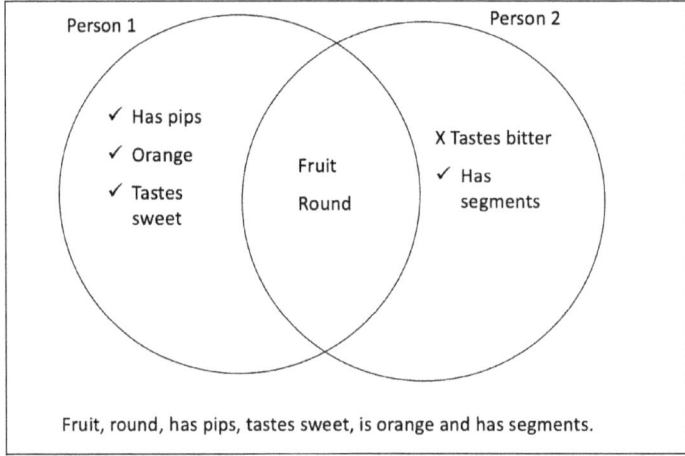

Now that you have two people in agreeance as to what an orange is, then you can compare it to another group's. Repeat the process until you have an agreed list between the whole group participating.

To put it in practical terms, for tennis fans or those who tune in after the group stage of major sporting tournaments, this part should be easy to follow. Essentially (in a neatly packaged world of 24 participants), the following shows what the process looks like to the point of one singular agreed hypothesis on what the topic is:

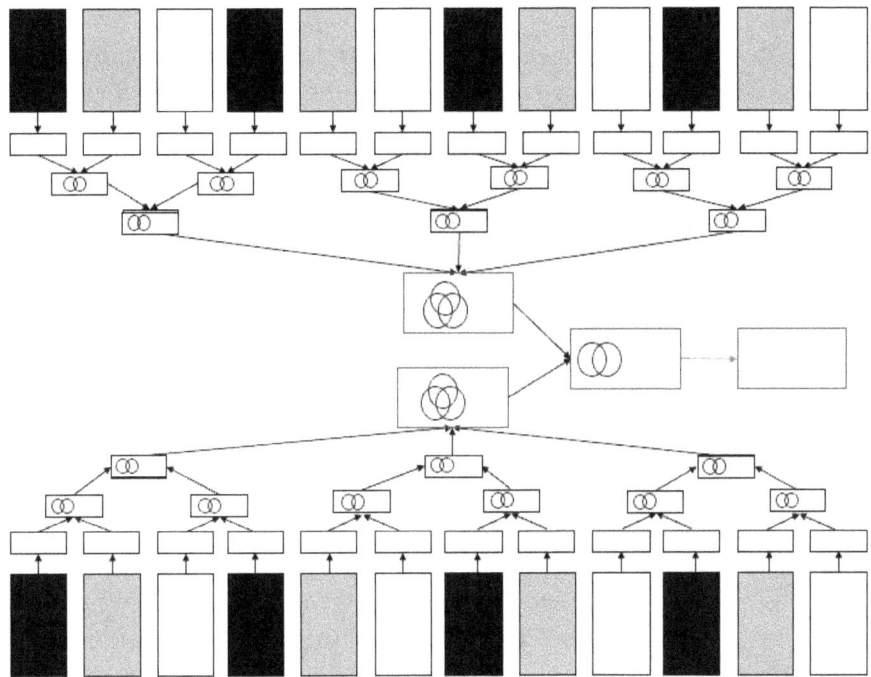

But I don't have 24 students, I have 17 and that is a prime number! What can I do? The number of students participating shouldn't have any bearing on your capacity to introduce this process. You may have to be slightly more strategic and pair students up to get easier to manipulate numbers. In the question above, simply pair two students together at the initial stage, and you have 16 – perfect!

But I have 29! Follow the same process as above, but simply pair more students together until you reach a desirable number. Even numbers tend to work best, but if you want Tri-Venn diagrams throughout, then go for it!

Who understands them?

If we applied this to the creation of maps in Mathematics or Geography, the outer vertical rectangles represent the stimulus. In which case, if you want your students to understand what makes a good map, then provide them with differing examples of maps. They could be Google maps, street directory, pirate's treasure maps, map of the school evacuation plan, etc. The stimulus (map) following the arrow leads to the individual articulation of what they believe a map needs.

The next level toward the middle is the first Venn diagram. This is where the individual students get together and compare their findings. They record their information in the Venn diagrams and then evaluate whether the unique items should be included or excluded. Space to write in this example is provided to the right of the Venn diagrams.

Moving one step closer to the middle provides the first opportunity for two groups of two students to join forces and compare four people's input. The process is exactly the same as the previous stage; except instead of comparing their original individual lists, they should be comparing what was decided upon while working in a pair.

The next stage is when things may get a touch tricky to manage. You may need to provide paper that is larger than a flashcard, but perhaps not. It would be prudent, however, to provide pre-printed templates to ensure there is adequate space to record in the Tri-Venn diagram. A further consideration is that you will have two groups of 12 students all attempting to engage (or disengage) from the same task. These students will be ready to compare and evaluate their answers. Anything they make as their list should be transferred onto individual Post-it notes.

Then the final one! I always advocate for raiding (with permission, of course) the PE storeroom and grabbing a couple of hula hoops. Place them in the centre of the classroom overlapped, as in a Venn diagram, and have the students sit on either side of the hoops. One student calls out their first item, then they either place it in the middle or in their section of the Venn diagram. The process follows until all are placed and evaluated. (If you are part of a school that has more than one class developing a rubric in this way, why not join together with your class's final one and another class's? Grab some chalk and draw a massive Venn diagram and have the students go through it again.)

Anything from the middle or that is agreed as being essential is now kept and lined up on the whiteboard. This is when the real evaluation and testing starts. But you need to have three more samples to test the list provided by the students. This is where you need a big space such as a whiteboard or wall space:

	Sample 1	Sample 2	Sample 3
☐			
☐			
☐			
☐			
☐			
☐			
☐			

Those Post-its have the writing from the students on them. Then, as a class, go through the first sample you are testing your thinking against. Under Sample 1, simply tick or cross your way through the sample:

	Sample 1	Sample 2	Sample 3
☐	✓		
☐	✓		
☐	✓		
☐	✓		
☐	✓		
☐	✓		
☐	✓		

It would be ideal if that was the case that everything we thought of was evident in that one sample. But due diligence is called for and the capacity to seek other samples will truly test our thinking. Now, repeat the process with two more samples in order to see whether the thinking measures up against multiple samples:

	Sample 1	Sample 2	Sample 3
☐	✓	✓	✓
☐	✓	✓	✓
☐	✓	✓	✓
☐	✓	✓	✓
☐	✓	✗	✗
☐	✓	✓	✓
☐	✓	✓	✓

In this instance, there is one item that has two crosses next to it. This is when you get to make a decision. Is the item worth keeping as it is important, or can the criteria be strong enough without it? (Consider if the samples you provided actually allowed for that criterion to be demonstrated or not.)

Now we have an agreed criterion of what a map looks like, you in essence have your success criteria (if you use Learning Intentions and Success Criteria, you are well on your way). These could also double as potential mini lessons, whole-class learning, teacher focus groups or student learning goals. How you use these outside the process of generating the rubric is entirely up to you; try not to limit yourself to a singular application of these rich morsels of potential learning.

Focusing on developing the rubric, I have found it advantageous to start with a blank starting point (digital document, whiteboard or butcher's paper). Then simply transfer the criterion developed earlier and place the first one in the middle column, as seen in the following table:

Working toward our criteria	Our criteria	Beyond our criteria
	Criterion 1...	
	Criterion 2...	

With that first criterion, the class needs to develop the statement fully. If working with the 'map' outlined earlier, it simply said 'Title', it would need to be fleshed out into prose that is assessable either qualitatively or quantitatively. In other words, make it into a sentence and measurable, for example, 'The title clearly matches the map'. This process must include the students in it; without them, how are they going to understand it and, at the end of the day, they are the ones who need to understand it better than teachers!

While in the headspace of developing this criterion, I then pivot sideways. There is no recipe for success by doing the working toward or beyond section, just articulate them both before moving to the next criterion:

Working toward our criteria	Our criteria	Beyond our criteria
The title doesn't accurately match the map	The title clearly matches the map	The title clearly matches the map and is centred at the top
	Criterion 2...	

Continue in this manner until you have fully fleshed out each criterion across the three levels. That will now be a completed rubric. Adding sections at the end of the rubric, such as level achieved, feedback (teacher/student/peer) or goal setting are advisable but entirely at your discretion. Your school may have a standard section added to rubrics that can be inserted also.

What a nice little neat package we've developed for that utopian classroom we exist in, where all students are neatly within measurable bands and unicorns run freely through the woods while elven characters nestle under mushroom caps. Snapping back to reality, what we have is a rubric that measures the bulk of our class.

Rubric horizon graph

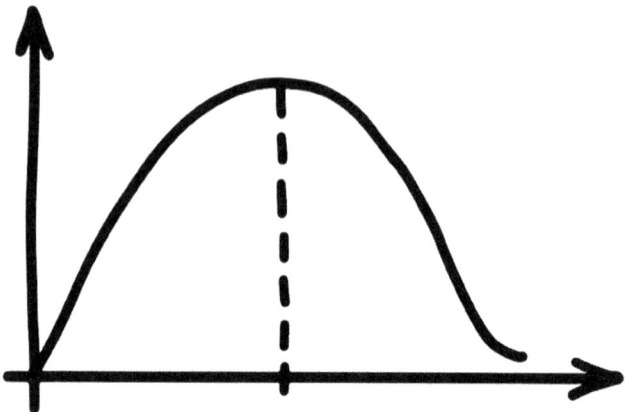

How do you assess those at the polar ends of the scale?

There are a few statistical outliers that exist in the world of sport – Sir Donald Bradman, Wayne Gretzky, Jack Nicklaus and David Campese, to name a few. We celebrated these statistical outliers, not as once in a lifetime or generation, but a 'once in ever' player. But there are players at the other end of the continuum that we question their selection, skill level or decision-making. Mercifully, this is not how we treat the statistical outliers in our classrooms.

We acknowledge there is a continuum of learners that are plotted everywhere possible. Then the question is: *How do we cater for our statistical outliers?* The notion of rubric horizons comes in when there are those at our extreme ends and can't demonstrate accurately their level of knowledge, skill or proficiency based on a three-levelled rubric. This is particularly important to consider if you are in a school where there are two grade levels engaging in the same learning (as is the case with many inquiries).

If you consider that students can be plotted at the 'standard', above or below, how far above and below are they? Have you consulted with the teachers or teams across the school to see if your idea of 'at standard' is consistent with their students? Imagine that you did all that work on maps in Grade 3 only to discover that when checking with the Grade 4 teacher, they have the exact same expectations. How can you say your students are at the standard for Grade 3, but yet if measured by the Grade 4 teacher they are still at standard?

It is pretty inexcusable for collaboration not to take place and ensure that there is a scope and sequence of learning across a school.

If you are working specifically with curriculum standards and you want to make the rubric as a professional and collaborative learning team, the process outlined earlier is still valid to follow with peers. However, the end product and how it is displayed may need to vary. The complexity of assessing when you have two grade levels engage in the same inquiry can be easily solved. Traditionally, when operating in collaborative teams, where the same content, skills and expectations are placed on the students, it would be fair and reasonable to assess like either of the below:

Below Standard	At Standard	Above Standard

Well Below Standard	Below Standard	At Standard	Above Standard	Well Above Standard

The limitation is that if you have Grade 3s and 4s, how can the standard be the same? One cohort has 12 months more schooling experience and should have higher expectations placed on them for the generic middle 'standard' of achievement.

One work around is creating separate rubrics, but there are limitations:

Well Below Standard Grade 3	Below Standard Grade 3	At Standard Grade 3	Above Standard Grade 3	Well Above Standard Grade 3

Well Below Standard Grade 4	Below Standard Grade 4	At Standard Grade 4	Above Standard Grade 4	Well Above Standard Grade 4

This would require high levels of communication, collaboration and adjustment. The work around is to abandon the notion of two tables and merge them into one. By doing this, it potentially minimises some of the discord:

Standards / Assessing...	Well Below Standard Grade 3	Below Standard Grade 3	At Standard Grade 3	Above Standard Grade 3	Well Above Standard Grade 3	
		Well Below Standard Grade 4	Below Standard Grade 4	At Standard Grade 4	Above Standard Grade 4	Well Above Standard Grade 4

The above demonstrates how you can merge the two from the beginning and see the progression of learning across age and stage. It may be the case that you wish to place more of a gap between the two 'standards'. If the curriculum documents for your location are set out in years, then it would be prudent to adopt to the below...

Standards / Assessing...	Well Below Standard Grade 3	Below Standard Grade 3	At Standard Grade 3	Above Standard Grade 3	Well Above Standard Grade 3		
			Well Below Standard Grade 4	Below Standard Grade 4	At Standard Grade 4	Above Standard Grade 4	Well Above Standard Grade 4

The absolute beauty of a rubric horizon is that there is no end! Just like a visual horizon, when driving long distances in the open, you can never reach the horizon; it continues out in front of you. How amazing to think that we are able to potentially design a rubric that has the capacity to measure learning wherever it falls, not just the confines of our scaffold. Our 'new' scaffold is flexible and adjusts to accommodate our statistical outliers. Instead of simply being marked well above standard, we could actually provide an accurate insight of how far ahead or the capacity to track themselves and aim for a target.

The work engaged here generally takes one of two flavours. The measurable differences between each stage are quantitative and qualitative. Both draw upon the wonderful world of cognitive verbs. Marzano and Kendall (2007) undertook significant research to develop a six-levelled taxonomy by further breaking down Bloom's Taxonomy (remembering that a taxonomy is based on research and is a tool developed as a result, so it is far greater than speculative or a theory). Marzano and Kendall broke down the six levels of Bloom's Taxonomy to provide a clear framework for teachers to map out and plan for the particular cognitive skills required by students to succeed at each level. For a great table on cognitive verbs the Queensland Curriculum and Assessment Authority has produced this helpful guide: www.qcaa.qld.edu.au/downloads/p_10/ac_categories_cognitive_verbs.pdf

For the example below, we will explore how to differentiate the following criterion in a rubric (using our horizons): *The different emotions we have.*

Quantitative differentiation

This is where each section is differentiated through quantity. The quality on a statement like this is number based around the amount of emotions that can be identified, stated or listed. Working with the words identified, stated and listed, these must be a part of the rubric, as these are the skills we are seeking our students to perform cognitively; therefore, they are cognitive verbs and are essential!

If we are requiring students to list, then our levels may look like this:

	Well Below Standard Grade 3	Below Standard Grade 3 Well Below Standard Grade 4	At Standard Grade 3 Below Standard Grade 4	Above Standard Grade 3 At Standard Grade 4	Well Above Standard Grade 3 Above Standard Grade 4	Well Above Standard Grade 4
The different emotions we have	Cannot **identify** any emotions	**Identify** one or two emotions	**Identify** three emotions	**Identify** four emotions	**Identify** five or more 'simple' emotions	**Identify** a wider nuanced range of emotions (at least five)

Qualitative differentiation

This is a different beast altogether, but still calls upon (more heavily this time) the use and support of cognitive verbs. This time, numbers don't enter the equation at all (pardon the pun). Could we measure and assess *The different emotions we have* qualitatively? The answer is yes:

	Well Below Standard Grade 3	Below Standard Grade 3 Well Below Standard Grade 4	At Standard Grade 3 Below Standard Grade 4	Above Standard Grade 3 At Standard Grade 4	Well Above Standard Grade 3 Above Standard Grade 4	Well Above Standard Grade 4
The different emotions we have	Cannot **identify** any emotions	**Identifies** a range of emotions	**Identifies and classifies** a range of emotions	**Identifies and describes** a range of emotions	**Investigates** how emotions differ	**Examines** the importance of emotions

Qualitative and quantitative differentiation

Why not do both? This sense of not throwing the baby out with the bathwater (what a bizarre turn of phrase) can fit quite neatly into the design of learning rubrics. Having a blend and balance of the two can be what is required to fully allow your students to demonstrate their learning:

	Well Below Standard Grade 3	Below Standard Grade 3 Well Below Standard Grade 4	At Standard Grade 3 Below Standard Grade 4	Above Standard Grade 3 At Standard Grade 4	Well Above Standard Grade 3 Above Standard Grade 4	Well Above Standard Grade 4
The different emotions we have	Cannot identify any emotions	Identifies one to five emotions	Identifies and classifies one to five emotions	Identifies and classifies six or more emotions	Identifies and describes one to five emotions	Identifies and describes six or more emotions

There is still clear differentiation and they are still measurable. The task here for teachers is to provide the space for such knowledge to be shared. Whether it is quantitative, qualitative or a combination of both, set your parameters, share them with the students and allow them to help guide their own learning trajectory.

Who assesses against them?

Teachers can. Students can. Peers can. Anyone who has access to the learning and the rubric can. The ideal is that the students are involved in it – after all, it is their learning being assessed. I always struggle with the notion of parent-teacher interviews where the student is absented. My issue here is: if in any industry you had a perform review or an annual review meeting and it was people talking about you and you were kept out of the conversation, that would be bizarre. So, why do we do it with students and their learning so often? Similarly, not providing students with a copy of the rubric does not include them, nor does it fully set them up for success.

When do you create them?

My belief has always been the earlier in the learning sequence you develop them, the more potential to be purposeful they are. Why not create them early so they can be formative and not just summative? Provide the transparency and set up your learners for success. It may even help you as a teacher to ensure that you are providing opportunities for the full range of the rubric to be assessed.

If you make and share the rubric at the end of the unit, you may find yourself in the awkward position of thinking, 'Hmmm, there is no point to creating anything that is above or well above, as the students didn't get to show that.' What a shame that would be to limit a group of students' learning as a result of the lack of pressing print or send!

Which direction do you go?

The direction you end up pursuing ultimately needs to be the right one for you and your team and is dependent upon your local context. If it is with students, with peers or a combination of both, that is what you need to decide in your setting. The important element is that you have created the rubrics and not relied on ones found online or resurrected versions from previous years.

Create them collaboratively, share them with your students and provide opportunities for all areas of the rubric to be evidenced through the learning experiences you provide your students.

Chapter summary

- Creating rubrics is a collaborative and dynamic process.
- Involve the students as much as practical and possible.
- Try the Think it Great™ process as it is collaborative and generates consistency of understanding and has the capacity to build from criteria to rubrics.
- Rubrics are typically hard-edged. The rubric horizon provides the opportunity to cater for those who perform at the extremities of the scope of learning.
- Rubrics can be created using qualitative or quantitate measures.
- If you are working across levels, consider 'merging' the rubrics to create a larger scope of potential to capture learning levels.
- Cognitive verbs can help to differentiate the rubric levels.

Reflection

Think about assessment in your school.

- **When is the assessment planned for?** Is it at the beginning, middle or end of the unit? Are they delivered to you in a neat package without ownership or are they developed by your team?
- **How are the assessment pieces identified?** Are they developed at the beginning of a sequence of learning? Or at the end? Do you have to create assessment pieces at the end of the inquiry to validate your rubric or your reporting indicators?
- **What does moderation look like for these pieces?** At some point, teams need to moderate. You can't have one teacher interpreting learning in one way and another teacher interpreting the same piece in another way. It simply isn't fair. How does your school deliver low levels of variability in assessment?
- **Do rubrics have horizons or edges?** If it is static, how will you demonstrate the capacity of your statistical outliers or even those who are slightly away from the mean on the standard deviation?

CHAPTER 9

PROVOCATIONS

"We only think when confronted with a problem"
– John Dewey (1933)

"I threw my head and my heart in the cockpit. The sounds of the engines. The voices from upstairs I only heard my crew. Preparing me for take-off. Preparing me"
– Something for Kate: 'Captain (Million Miles an Hour)'

This chapter will explore the different ways we can engage students in provocations and with the right amount of consideration and planning to capture their hearts and minds. Provocations, although difficult to attribute to a time, have been in education since the early 1900s first introduced by Maria Montessori. Yes, more than a hundred years ago – and here we are thinking we are doing something new and wonderful. We are actually currently close to being a quarter of the way through the 21st century, so can we please stop saying we are preparing learning for the 21st century?

Provocations, when used in a primary school setting, are based on the idea that children learn best when they are actively engaged in the learning process and are encouraged to explore and discover on their own. This is done by creating an environment that encourages curiosity, creativity and exploration; teachers can help students develop critical thinking skills, problem-solving abilities and a love of learning that will serve them well throughout their lives.

This chapter will explore the following topics:
- **Sensory learning**
- **Content-based and conceptual provocations**
- **Provocations across the curriculum**

- Provocations with staff
- The right ingredients
- Capturing hearts and minds

Sensory learning

Smell

As a child growing up, we would travel each summer somewhere in regional Victoria. Most often we would head toward the Murray River and spend time fishing. We would go on tours of places I had little to no interest in and visit various places I have no recollection of. It wasn't until years later, as an adult, I went to the Barossa Valley that I was hit with a flood of memories – my own personal Proustian moment – all through the power of smell.

"This should not be surprising, as neuroscience makes clear. Smell and memory seem to be so closely linked because of the brain's anatomy…" (*The Harvard Gazette*, 2020). There are many triggers that we have: walking into a rustic pub has a smell all of its own, a bakery, the fish section at a market, etc. But I wonder how sensory sterile our classrooms are when it comes to the olfactory sense? We talk of hands-on learning, which is wonderful, but do we talk of engaging the other senses as much? I have never heard of nose-on learning, but perhaps there's a case for it…

When writing, we encourage our students to write using all five senses, exploring through their creativity what they see, hear, touch, taste and smell. But how many of these opportunities do they get to engage in through their everyday learning? They will see many things, hear many things and touch many things. But taste and smell seem to be the poor cousins of sense when it comes to education and learning. And it makes me wonder why. Why, when the sense of smell is the most closely linked to memory, do we not engage it more so in classrooms? But smell is not all we need to focus on. There are four other senses and their hearts and minds.

Touch

In preschools and kindergartens, there are sensory boxes – or touch boxes – to stimulate and engage learners. We see it on TV shows like *I'm a Celebrity… Get Me Out of Here*, where the celebrities blindly put their hands or other body parts in areas they can't see and are challenged by what they touch. Some of these are harmless, others not, but their minds play tricks on them and they misinterpret the sensory data coming in. The power of touch is immense.

McGlone and Walker (2021) found key benefits to hugs, one being, "Touch provides the 'glue' that holds us together, underpinning our physical and emotional wellbeing." Not that I'm advocating for going out and hugging your students or staff tomorrow, but the power of touch cannot be underestimated. We hear of hands-on learning and play-based learning becoming increasingly important in the role of learning. There are lessons to be learned here and we can make changes to our classrooms to incorporate more sensory learning.

Taste

With occupational health and safety, food safety and allergies prominent in schools, this one requires some careful consideration and planning. Taste can be a powerful tool for provoking emotions and memories, which can really enhance the learning experience and help to make information more meaningful and memorable. Williams and Penman (2011) talk of mindful eating and this has recently been introduced into primary classrooms through the practice of 'The Chocolate Meditation'. As teachers, we would certainly benefit from mindfulness and meditation. As humans with chocolate… I'll leave you to fill in the blank!

We know that taste and smell are linked (they are actually controlled by the same part of the brain), so how can you link the sense of taste to your provocations?

Sight

Pictures are worth a thousand words – so use them. There are so many rich, powerful and thought-provoking images that can stimulate student learning. Most schools currently use these to great effect, layering them and carefully ordering them, which can be an important step also. When an artist sets up a gallery; a curator sets up a museum display; or a landscape gardener places plants exactly where they want them, know that there is intention and thought behind each of these. They are designed to draw you in further or take you on a journey or sequenced for maximum visual effect. Consider how you might use visuals in your provocations.

Hearing

Audio clips and songs are incredible ways to stimulate and provoke learning. Listening to a powerful speech or oration can change how we interpret information. Said with the right inflection, tone and intonation, voice is a powerful tool to use.

Playing soundscapes is a powerful way to immerse your students into a setting – you needn't tell them where they are or what they will hear, just that they will hear sounds. Their task is to be present in the learning experience.

The use of music to provoke emotions is not new. We needn't get carried away here with the Mozart effect, as there is no conclusive evidence to prove its effectiveness. What I'm advocating for here is the use of music as a provocation – not a memory aid or an enhancement to learning.

Use songs with lyrics that have a message, theme or concept that is related to what you are studying – but be careful to read the lyrics thoroughly! Finding contemporary music that resonates with your students may be advantageous as they already like and know the song. Musicians are artists, and they have chosen to express themselves through the power of song. What is expressed usually means something of significance to the writer and designed to engage with an audience. Choose the right pieces that will 'speak' to your audience.

Instrumental tracks can be equally powerful, using the instrumentation only to elicit feelings, moods or imagery. Movies and TV shows have soundtracks to them that are quite often instrumental – there are more than 18 hours of original music in the Star Wars movies and about four of them have lyrics. I'd guess most people could recognise the Star Wars themes than could sing along with 'Duel of the Fates' in *Star Wars: Episode 1 – The Phantom Menace*. That anthemic Star Wars theme captures the essence of the franchise and is instantly recognisable.

Disney's *Fantasia* uses classical tracks from Bach, Tchaikovsky, Dukas, Stravinsky, Beethoven, Ponchielli, Mussorgsky and Schubert. There are no spoken words through the movie. It uses the music and the visuals to tell the tale. The sequence of *The Sorcerer's Apprentice* is immeasurably enhanced by the music.

Music can do amazing things, so how will you use it to enhance the learning through provocations?

Content-based and conceptual provocations

Traditionally, teachers limit their students to content-based provocations. They are ways of exploring the content and getting the student familiar with the idea that they are hooked into the topic and will want to learn more about the inquiry. These are a brilliant way to engage students at any stage through an inquiry. Excursions, guest speakers and incursions are perfect examples of content-based provocations that are highly effective (provided we get the right ones). If you are exploring businesses and work, bring in a parent who is a business owner or a local business owner and have them speak in real terms. If you are fortunate, you may be able to visit a business and see first-hand. These are powerful ways to get an insight, and far more powerful than a quick search on the internet for a premade video that gets close to suiting the purpose. You get out what you put in – and what you may get out is students that are partially or not at all engaged. More powerfully stated, your students get out what you put in.

If we are spending time on deciding on the concepts that frame an inquiry or that are related and guide where the learning is going, a case can be made for provocations being conceptual in nature. Hypothetically, you could have an inquiry with the key understanding being: *'Innovation and planning support the running of successful businesses,'* then you can go with content-based provocations or conceptual provocations.

Content-based provocations would be looking at businesses, perhaps different business models or business processes and systems, whereas you could go down the conceptual provocation lens and explore the concepts related to this as you would have already identified and documented them. If one of the related concepts was function (as you are looking at how businesses function), then you are free to explore function in any way you wish – no longer bound by content. The possibilities are limited only by your imagination.

Why not try out the teabag rocket experiment? A simple online search will provide the links to clips or directions. Canvassed to get the students thinking and doing (hands-on) and interacting with each other (interpersonal), it is a fun experiment to try. Set up the provocation by asking the students to design a rocket only using a teabag and explaining how it functions/works. While the students are experimenting and ideally engaged, explicitly use the word 'function' in your interactions with them. Remind them you need to know how it functions, and ask how it will function, etc. Once the activity is complete, it is important to debrief and reinforce the nature of function in the activity, otherwise it was just a fun activity with no connection to their learning.

A beautiful text by Meg McKinlay (2020) titled *How to Make a Bird* could be a different way to explore the concept of function, as the book outlines what is needed to make a bird. This could be read to students, with discussions after sections or pages centred on function or how things work. There are so many ways to explore function through this picture storybook (or so many others).

MC Escher's (1928) piece titled *Tower of Babel* is a woodcut of the biblical story of the people of Babel attempting to build a tower to reach God (google it). It is clear to see that there has been a miscommunication in how the building was built. Something went wrong in the process, something stopped functioning. Someone stopped functioning. Explore this with the students and see what they can come up with – but keep bringing an explicitness back to function.

Conceptual provocations are often used in inquiry-based learning approaches, where students are encouraged to investigate, analyse and reflect on complex ideas and problems. They can take many forms, such as a visual image, a piece of text, a video or a real-world scenario, and are designed to generate discussion, debate and critical thinking.

An example of a conceptual provocation

As a school's pedagogical leader, I was working with teaching teams to ensure that provocations were conceptually based. The notion of teaching through concepts, as you may have realised by now, is something that is very much a part of my own teaching philosophy.

At the beginning of a new inquiry, the Grade 5 classroom teacher was on leave, so that provided an opportunity to involve the students in a new learning direction. Exploring the notion that *'Living things need to adapt in order to survive,'* one of our related concepts was adaptation. Knowing that adaptation was naturally going to occur in the classroom due to a change of teacher, I thought that the best concept for initial exploration.

Before launching the unit, I repositioned all of the tables in the room and removed all of the chairs. I wrote a note on the board welcoming the students as learners and invited them to embrace the difference. Upon entering the classroom, the students were confronted with an unfamiliar environment. They began to express concern about how they could learn in that space. Anticipating this, I asked them to follow me to a different place to learn. We went outside to explore various locations, and it was not long before they were ready to express their thoughts on these new learning conditions. One of these conditions was the sports shed – it was not a popular or comfortable choice!

We re-entered the classroom to find it had been altered again (thanks to a colleague). I then let them know it was an adaptation exercise. The students reflected on this and began to ask more questions about why this was happening. Together, we worked to refine their inquiries.

In the next few days, activities were designed for the students to provoke adaptation to new ways of working. I deliberately ensured that the adaptation exercises encompassed different learning content areas. I wanted to reinforce the integrated nature of inquiry learning without the barriers of curriculum names.

The students experienced and learned more about the concept of adaptation and were better placed to start tackling the subject of living things adapting to their environment. Not only were they able to experience what adaptation felt like, but they could recall from their own experiences how different factors change or affect the type or duration of adaptation.

Provocations across the curriculum

We can truly make learning memorable and powerful for our students if we carefully select and design learning opportunities that engage all their senses and their hearts and minds. Will these provocations capture each student the same way? Possibly not. Yet, we tend to use this technique sparingly and only in the realm of inquiry. It has always troubled me that teachers I engage with limit the use of provocations or multisensory learning purely to inquiry and never in Literacy or Maths. When asking why, I've never received an answer that I can walk away with and think that I'm comfortable with.

Teachers can and do plan incredible provocations to engage their students. Limiting this to inquiry makes as much sense to cooking a five-course dinner and focusing so much on the entrées that they are Michelin-star restaurant quality, then the next four courses are neglected and don't match the effort or beauty of the entrée. Why is it that we develop these incredible provocations in one area of learning but not others? More importantly than answering that, is when are we going to start to use provocations in all learning areas? Our inquiry planners even have a section explicitly dedicated to tuning in/provocations/engaging. When will we transfer this highly effective style of learning to the rest of our curriculum? Hopefully the answer is soon, as the potential engagement and learning these present is worth the investment of time, energy and thought.

Think about how you introduce fractions, decimals and percentages. This has the potential to be quite dry and may not be the most enthralling learning that a student may engage in. So, try to make it interesting! Make it something they want to learn more about. A quick online search suggests there are amazing decimal activities that your students will love. The same is true for percentages and fractions. Strangely, fractions seem to have the most hands-on activities offered, when in essence they are all related as different ways of expressing parts of a number.

If you can, get food involved. What is pizza cut into (and no, the answer isn't slices)? It could be expressed as eighths – or it could be expressed as 0.125 or 12.5%. If you phone pizza shops, they will deliver unsliced pizzas. A block of chocolate is broken up into parts that can easily be broken apart. Buy a few blocks and get the students to be hands-on (or gloves-on). Incentivise the learning – if they correctly identify a certain amount or can demonstrate certain knowledge or skills, they can eat it!

If food isn't for your students (chocolate and pizza should be a reasonably safe bet, however), then you could change gears entirely and do a word study – not as much fun for some, but for others this may be the light-bulb moment. Explore words related to fraction, decimal and percentage, and explore their etymologies, as in the following table:

Word	Word meaning	Etymology	Related words
Fraction	A numerical quantity that is not a whole number	*fractio* (a breaking, especially into pieces)	fracture, fractal, fractious, fragile
Decimal	Relating to or denoting a system of numbers and arithmetic based on the number 10, tenth parts, and powers of 10	*decem* (meaning 10)	decade, decapod, December, decathlon, decimate, decuple
Percentage	A rate, number or amount in each hundred	*per centum* (by the hundred)	cent, century, centurion, centimetre, centenary

Students tend to love a story and are generally great audiences if you can keep them entertained. Ask them to tell you a story or tell your own of when a bone was fractured; bring in an X-ray to show what it looks like. It is something that used to be whole, broken into pieces. Bring in something fragile (not valuable, perhaps take a quick trip to a second-hand store to buy a vase) and demonstrate its fragility. It will break into smaller parts. Being explicit with the words fragile, fraction and fracture will hopefully link the learning.

Think of all the words related to deci – December (it used to be the tenth month), decade, decathlon, decapod, etc. Ten (or deci) is such an important number in our Mathematics history. Our numbers are base 10 (or base deci), because we have 10 fingers! Anything grouped in 10s is related to deci. How could you explore this with your students?

Percentages have so many links to explore either through per or cent. Looking at cent, the obvious link is through dollars and cents. But could you explore the following with your students:

- How many soldiers (or legionaries) was a **cent**urion in charge of? 100
- How many **cent**imetres in a metre? 100
- How many years in a **cent**ury? 100
- What is it called when a batter in cricket makes 100 runs? A **cent**ury

Making all these links with the word **cent** can only reinforce the students' knowledge of percentage. Using any of the above stories will help their knowledge of fractions, decimals and percentages, but they won't do the *teaching* of them. But you may have captured their imaginations or at least got them sitting up and paying attention to the words and have a deeper understanding of what the words mean to support their next steps in using them.

Provocations with staff

Teachers are learners, too – we are often forgotten as learners, though. Don't we then also deserve the opportunity to get excited and engaged about our learning? Yes, yes, yes. The challenge is then, what do we do about it? Some areas are harder than others, and with time constraints they can be challenging to either find the time to plan or deliver. But they could just be the investment you need to get staff on board with the learning.

I may be one of the few people who genuinely loves moderating writing samples. I just find the richness and the robust nature of collegial discord so invigorating. The learning that comes from these sessions is incredible and I sincerely look forward to them. But I fear I am in the minority. When leading these sessions, I try to find ways to engage the staff in the headspace required. Recently, I used a clip from YouTube to stimulate thinking of what not to do when moderating. It outlines the marking strategy that is questionable and less than valid. But it was a great way to discuss the protocols we would operate under. www.youtube.com/watch?v=0fn_vAhu_Lw

When I was working with a middle school team, they requested a professional learning on sentence structures. Now, that has the potential to be quite vanilla and bland. Somehow, in the preceding weeks, I'd discovered a series of clips made by a ridiculously talented individual: Lubalin. His series titled 'Turning Random Internet Drama Into Songs' was able to be used to highlight the difference between the written word and the spoken word, the importance of punctuation and identifying different sentence structures – plus, it was hilarious.

When conducting professional learning on spelling, I wanted to challenge the thinking in the room and really get staff cognitively active. Together we watched a clip of a highly efficient speller – search 'Spelling Bee Numb Nut'. That was great to stimulate thinking, but I wanted to get inside the teachers' heads and find out their thoughts. I didn't want to have dominant voices, so I used the Chalk Talk protocol. The statements used were:

- People judge you based on your ability to spell.
- A schwa is the most common vowel sound in English.
- Some people are naturally good at spelling.
- An example of a derivational morpheme is 'ly'.
- Spelling needs to be explicitly taught.
- Entomology is the study of word origins.
- Quingraphs are the largest group of graphs.
- English spelling has no discernible pattern.
- Spelling is hard.

This stimulated a lot of pen and paper discussion, but after the protocol was finished, we engaged in great conversations. None would have been as deep or as rich if there hadn't been provocations at the beginning to stimulate their thinking.

When working with a senior team conducting some professional learning about inquiry learning, I decided to bring my guitar along to the session and find some clips to support the learning. As a novice (and that is being kind) at playing the guitar, I knew the chords to a few songs, which I found the clips for, along with the clip of Tash Sultana's 'Welcome to the Jungle' and David Ford's 'State of the Union'. We started off with the question of what is looping? There were different responses – most were reasonably accurate, but none picked up on the musical definition. Then we watched Tash Sultana's clip and suddenly there were light-bulb moments of 'Oh, that could be looping'. We discussed, watched David Ford's clip and landed on a new working definition.

Then the question was given to the team: did they want to learn how to play a song? The answer – mercifully – was yes. So, I grabbed my guitar and gave them a choice of songs to learn the chords to. Thankfully, they chose the classic 'Ice Ice Baby' by Vanilla Ice. But the twist in the tail was that I wasn't going to teach them – they would have to learn to play it themselves, through trial and error, discovery and giving each other feedback and advice. It didn't take long. In the end, they could play the piece of music that could be looped over to form the bassline for the song.

After the experience of learning to play a looped set of chords on a guitar, we discussed how this paralleled to inquiry learning. The conversation was so rich and active. Normally quieter members were animated and actively participating in the conversation. It was successful in that the activity did the teaching on my behalf – all I had to do was a bit of thinking beforehand and resource it appropriately.

Staff deserve these types of experiences with learning. We cannot expect teachers to go into their classrooms and try all these provocations and take risks if we, as leaders, are not modelling it to them. Have a think about what you could do to engage your staff through a provocation before the next time you meet with them.

The right ingredients

I'm no chef – and have never claimed to be. But there is the simple notion of, if you use the right ingredients, you get good results. But knowing what to do with the ingredients is equally important. Simply having raw ingredients is not sufficient for success. Or knowing what to do but not having the right ingredients is equally problematic.

If handed an ounce of black caviar, some small pancakes, dill, red onion, sour cream and an egg, I wouldn't have a clue what to do with them. But if someone said, "You need to make Black Russian Caviar", I'd do a quick search online to find the recipe and dutifully follow the steps. It would be very manual and forced, with no fluency or flow to my preparation. And the end product, well, it just wouldn't be as aesthetically pleasing enough for anyone to attempt to eat. My wife, on the other hand, will open the fridge or pantry door and find raw ingredients and create a meal without a recipe or experience; she has the confidence and expertise to know what works and what doesn't work. She tests as she goes along, tasting, adding more of this or that, responding to what is in front of her. Isn't that what great teachers do?

But if you have the ingredients and know what to do with them, that should be enough, right? Sometimes yes and sometimes no. There is a real skill and craft behind being able to create a delicious meal or an engaging provocation. They simply don't just materialise through hope or luck; they are crafted, trialled and refined. But having the wrong ingredients will never bring you success – you can't make a lemon meringue pie without lemon juice. That is why we must invest time, energy and thought into developing provocations that are designed to stimulate, challenge and engage students.

We learn from our mistakes; we get better at what we are attempting. We have some backslides in there, but we recognise what works well and what doesn't work. The interesting part of teaching is what works on one day in one class may not work at all in a different class on the same day. We need to constantly reflect and adjust to ensure the learning suits the learners we have. We have the privilege and responsibility of framing the inquiries at the beginning of the unit through the questions you ask and/or the provocations you provide. This can also be seen as the opportunity to model explicitly the asking of open-ended, driving questions that will promote conceptual development.

Capturing hearts and minds

You don't look at the leaves to find the problem with a tree – you do a full root and stem examination. Nor do you capture all learners fully through only engaging either their hearts or minds – it needs to be both. There is a synergy between provocations that are content-based, conceptual and impact the students' senses, hearts and minds. The more we can develop learning experiences that reach students in these ways, the more linked their cognitive and affective domain are. And the greater we impact their thinking and their feelings, the more potential we have for creating a change within them as learners. There is a richness and much to gain from developing these to capture the hearts and minds of our students.

But please, do not organise your provocations for the beginning of the inquiry and then leave them at that. Provocations can be planned and placed at any stage through an inquiry. Yes, they make a world of sense at the beginning of the inquiry when we are trying to capture students' attention and engage them in the new learning. Take the time to consider when else provocations could be used to enhance the learning. If you break your inquiries into smaller parts (mini inquiries), then do you engage them in each of these separately or into the inquiry in general? If your inquiry is not going well, do you plough ahead and hope that the students catch on, or could you pause and design a new provocation to attempt to recapture their interest?

Be considered in your timing and use of your provocations, and feel liberated to use them when you feel necessary. Use them often, use them in inquiry, use them in other subject or content areas, use them with your staff. Use them or lose them – and the 'them' I refer to here is the students and their engagement.

Chapter summary

- Sensory learning is powerful and we need to imagine ways to incorporate it into our daily learning experiences we offer students.
- Provocations are an important part of the learning process. We need to use them mindfully and strategically.
- Provocations can be content-based or conceptual in nature – and there is a valid reason for either at different times.
- Provocations needn't be limited to the beginning of an inquiry – used intentionally and creatively, they can be placed into any stage of learning.
- Inquiry isn't the 'owner' of provocations, so why not explore using them across the curriculum? They can be effective with any 'subject' or learning domain.
- Teachers are learners, too, so why not use provocations with their professional learning?
- Learning is far more than a cognitive experience; it enters the affective domain and we need to design learning to capture the hearts and minds of the students we teach.

Reflection

Connect. Extend. Challenge.

Using the Connect, Extend, Challenge thinking routine from Project Zero will guide the reflection. The routine supports students to make connections between new learnings and what they already know.

Think about provocations and how they look in your classroom.

- **Connect:** What do provocations currently look like in your classroom? What ideas or thoughts from this chapter can you connect with?
- **Extend:** What new ideas have you come across that have changed your thinking? What new directions have you been extended in?
- **Challenge:** What is challenging? Do you have any new questions? How would you go about answering those questions?

CHAPTER 10

HONOURING STUDENT VOICE

"Agency is the power to take meaningful and intentional action, and acknowledges the rights and responsibilities of the individual, supporting voice, choice and ownership…"
– **International Baccalaureate Organization (2017)**

"Look at me. I just can't believe what they've done to me. We could never get free. I just wanna be. I just wanna dream"
– **Major Lazer featuring Amber Dawn Coffman: 'Get Free'**

I'm not sure where I heard it first, but I love the statement 'If you don't want to know the answer, then don't ask the question'. In teaching, this is so painfully true when we consider student voice. When trying to explain student voice, it is important to understand what you want student voice to sound and look like in your school. And I mean to really think and consider what you want it to be.

Tokenism is so easy, it is a safe space to simply say, "We value student voice". But what do you, as a school, proactively, intentionally and transparently do about this?

At what level does the student voice come in? For some schools, districts and systems, there are limitations imposed that ultimately impact the emergence of student voice. This chapter is not going to explore all the ways in which student voice can be garnered; moreover, it is a simple approach to help you build student voice at a classroom level, which ensures that voices are heard and factored into the directions of the learning.

There are some schools doing amazing ground-breaking things with student voice, where the students are involved in every facet of their learning – not just the classroom, but planning with teachers and offering inputs or having entire ownership of their learning; powerful learning is happening! My experiences have never been full-blown student voice where the curriculum is entirely owned by the students, so I can't write about it. Nor is it fair to quote and paraphrase some experts and slap a couple of pages around it to make it sound as though this has been what I've done. Even worse, jump on to ChatGPT and smash out a quick chapter. But what I can speak from is the experiences I've had, the trial and error, the limitations I've faced and what I do differently as a result of the experiences.

This chapter will explore a variety of ways, through tweaking what many teachers currently do, to ensure that student voice is heard in some capacity in an inquiry.

This chapter is broken down into the following sections:

- **Harnessing a KWL**
- **Reviewing the teacher and student roles**
- **Communication vehicles**
- **Vacate the space (better yet, plan for it)**
- **Trust**
- **Heutagogy**

Harnessing a KWL

Have you ever been to a professional learning day or conference plenary and the speaker has asked questions from the audience? It is a great opportunity for interaction and the capacity to have some of your thinking or learning clarified. The questions that you ask will obviously determine the response you get, so you make it count. You will probably only get the one. But could you imagine if you asked your question and it was duly ignored and some other different content was introduced? You would feel reasonably aggrieved or upset that your question was ignored. Mercifully, that is not our reality (or at least not in my experience).

But what happens when we think we are attending to student voice or agency by asking them if they have any wonderings? The classic KWL – what I **Know**, **Want** to know and what I have **Learnt** – is a brilliant strategy for eliciting questions from students. It should be used to have the students record what they already know about a topic/concept/learning area. That should ultimately mean we don't need to waste their time by covering that content. The logical step that enhanced this was to add a 'H' in there – KWHL – **How** will I find out. This built in slightly more accountability and structure for students, but in the end... if it is primarily used at the start or the end of an inquiry, you could have 37 columns and it would make no difference (aside from the waste of time and paper).

A simple and traditional KWL, as seen below, allows the students to record under each heading. It is generally accompanied with a heading that is either the inquiry name or focus question/statement:

Title of the inquiry here:		
What do I **KNOW**?	What do I **WANT** to know?	What have I **LEARNT**?

But what if you played with the simple structure of a KWL and instead of it being three simple columns, you made it a matrix or a cross-classification chart? This can be done, as seen in the table below, with the addition of the mini inquiries/understandings/outcomes/lines of inquiry/focus statements (or any other term you use) in the left-hand column. Now, suddenly, the students are no longer inquiring into such a broad topic, but they are refined, and their thinking guided into areas that are within the confines of the inquiry.

Gasp, shock and horror! How dare I harness students' capacities and limit their questioning to where they want to go? Surely this is blasphemy?! In an increasingly accountable and litigious society that we operate in, think of these as a structure that will support agency along with ensuring that you add breadth and depth to the curriculum:

Title of the inquiry here:			
Area of focus	What do I **KNOW**?	What do I **WANT** to know?	What have I **LEARNT**?
Ways people behave in different weather conditions			
Natural cycles (seasons) impact the weather			
Tools we use to observe and measure weather			

An alternate version of a KWL, still using the attributes down the side, is to revisit them regularly. One trap that many teachers have fallen into is the notion of completing the K and the W sections at the beginning of the inquiry. The next step is to engage in the inquiry (teach it), then drag the KWL out of the depths of a student's desk, and at the end of the inquiry have the students dutifully complete the L section.

Why do we wait? Why not check in regularly with what their new questions are? Why not find out what they have learnt more regularly? This sense of formative assessment to gauge where you should invest your energy as a teacher (or with which individuals) is an important part of maintaining student voice in an inquiry – but you must act on it, not just ask for it.

The table below demonstrates how you could capture student thinking via a KWL each fortnight. You could explore this with greater or less regularity depending on your context:

Area of focus		What do I **KNOW**?	What do I **WANT** to know?	What have I **LEARNT**?
Ways people behave in different weather conditions	Week 1			
	Week 3			
	Week 5			
	Week 7			
Natural cycles (seasons) impact the weather	Week 1			
	Week 3			
	Week 5			
	Week 7			
Tools we use to observe and measure weather	Week 1			
	Week 3			
	Week 5			
	Week 7			

It may be a bit too busy – consider breaking them into three separate parts. Break them up by the area of focus. That way, you can ensure that there is space for each student to record their thinking and it not be clouded or confused by the 'noise' of the other areas of focus. The two tables below represent alternate ways to present the KWL to students.

Version 1. Split into three distinct areas with the area of focus at the top:

Ways people behave in different weather conditions			
Area of focus	What do I **KNOW**?	What do I **WANT** to know?	What have I **LEARNT**?
Week 1			
Week 3			
Week 5			
Week 7			

Version 2. This includes the area of focus into the KWL prompts:

	What do I **KNOW** about *ways people behave in different weather conditions*?	What do I **WANT** to know about *ways people behave in different weather conditions*?	What have I **LEARNT** about *ways people behave in different weather conditions*?
Week 1			
Week 3			
Week 5			
Week 7			

For something slightly different, removing the content (areas of focus) from the thinking, you could create a KWL focusing on conceptual understanding. Depending on how you plan, you may or may not identify concepts that tie the learning together. This isn't a reference to major thematic concepts that inquiries are planned around (though you could do that also); these are the inquiry-specific conceptual foci that you plan for.

Using the areas of focus on the previous pages, we will extract the concept from them. When planning, I prefer to start with a concept, then build the area of focus, but in this instance, it will work for illustrative purposes.

Ways people behave in different weather conditions – this is behavioural or about how things work or about causal relationships; in other words, cause and effect. Let's call this one cause and effect.

Natural cycles (seasons) impact the weather – this could be about cycles, patterns, rhythms or cause and effect, relationships, connection. For this example, we will go with relationships.

Tools we use to observe and measure weather – this is really about different types of forms. The concept could be form or classification or type. For this example, we'll use type.

Now that you have concepts identified, all the incarnations of KWLs as outlined previously are equally valid, and it's up to you to choose which one would work best. Using concepts on your KWL will only work if you are explicit with the concepts themselves and the students have a functional understanding of them. If they don't, the organiser could be unsuccessful as the students don't know how to engage with them. Be explicit, name them. Explicitly say the concepts often and in context. When looking at how natural cycles impact weather, use the word, relationships, often.

If you don't, you may get some very interesting thinking recorded by your students in some of these boxes!

	What do I **KNOW** about?	What do I **WANT** to know about?	What have I **LEARNT** about?
Cause and effect			
Relationships			
Type			

Massive divergent segue warning: I love kimchi, the Korean food. The strength of flavour and sharpness just make it amazing for me. I went through a phase of eating it – a lot! But I overdid it. I went too hard and the freshness of it wasn't there anymore. It is a cautionary culinary tale that I tell to warn you off doing KWLs all the time with every inquiry or learning area. You run the risk of stultification and ensuring that the unique loses its impact, and your students disengage. The same can be said of many graphic organisers or pedagogical techniques.

The other way to work with KWLs (or other such strategies to gain an insight into the learning and questions students have) is to collect them. Bring them back to the planning table. If your school doesn't have the structures or desire (no judgements on either) to have students actually involved in the planning stage, then do the next best thing: bring their thinking. We have a responsibility to listen to the students' voices and what it is they are learning or are interested in learning. Bringing their KWLs (or other) to planning ensures that even though they are physically absent, their thinking is present.

How you factor in their thinking and questioning is up to you. Try and aggregate their questions into groups. Identify if there is a pattern to the thinking and questions they have. If there are patterns that emerge, consider how you best respond to them. Do you explicitly plan for them or provide time and space for them to be explored by students?

Reviewing the teacher and student roles

Take a moment to get out the inquiry process that you use. Write the stages of the inquiry process down a page and place a line next to each of them. Consider this line to be a line that represents the potential control that you or the students have over their learning during each phase as a percentage. Place a marker down where you believe it to be true of that stage of an inquiry in your classroom. In the example below, you can see that everything to the left of the x represents the time where the teacher is in control of the learning, and everything to the right is where the student is in control of their learning.

For example:

Tuning In	_____x_____
Finding Out	_____x_____
Sorting Out	_____x_____
Going Further	_____x_____
Making Conclusions	_____x_____
Taking Action	_____x_____

Does the above example ring true for you? Does it look similar to what you put? This example is illustrative only and not what I am advocating for, but if this is where you are at, this is where you are at. What we want to achieve is progress and change – no one goes to a doctor hoping to come out feeling the same. We want improvement, which is what this book aims to support – your development and improvement.

Will you focus on moving one of the x marks you plotted against a particular phase? Will you go for more or all? That is entirely up to you; setting a goal is key. Hattie (2009) states that "goal setting is a powerful form of agency as it enables students to take ownership of their learning" (p. 29). He also states that goal setting should be guided by educators, who help students set challenging but achievable goals, and provide ongoing support and feedback to help students reach their goals.

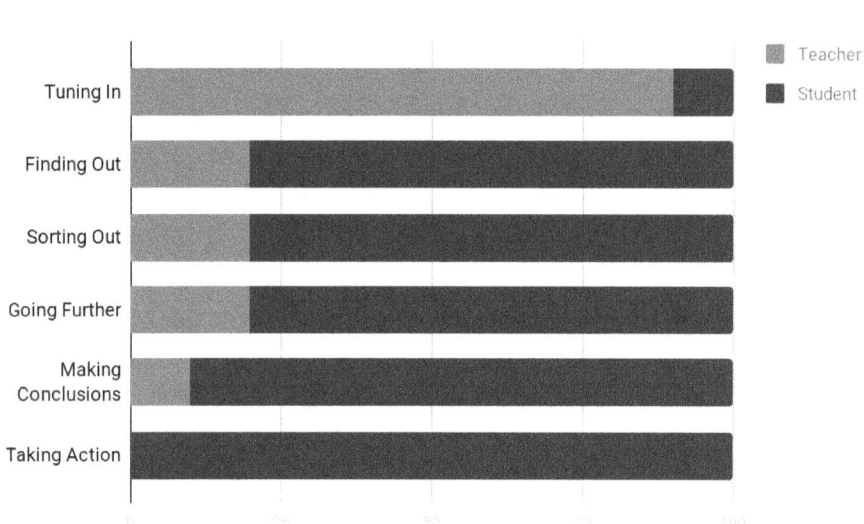

Who in control of the learning?

This model reflects what I believe the 'balance' of control looks like across an inquiry. How does this compare to your reality or desired reality? Is it the same across your team, your level or your school? It may be an important pedagogical conversation to have in your school.

Communication vehicles

These are simply ways that students can share their learning. Brainstorm a list of different ways students can share their learning. Make sure this is a dynamic display that can be added to or have items removed from. Make sure that it is the students that are coming up with ideas and not just ones that we, as teachers, are hoping for.

With a list of different ways to share their learning visible in the classroom, it opens up possibilities for students to choose their own 'how'. There may be ideas that they may never have thought of previously, but this has enabled them to try something new.

But *what happens when a student keeps using the same strategy or tool to communicate their learning?* If you are seeking to challenge students to trial new or different ways to present their learning, then you may wish to create a chart to audit their choices.

Charting student choices table

	Claymation	Diorama	Website	Piece for assembly	Letter to	PowerPoint	Make a movie	Write a song	Create an exhibit
Student 1									
Student 2									
Student 3									
Student 4									

Vacate the space (better yet, plan for it)

Meetings, when organised, run to a simple formula: welcome, go through the agenda, clarify, general business, confirm the next meeting date and say goodbye. Meetings without an agenda can be an awkward space to be in. There's less accountability, more space for opinions and random topics being brought up. They can be very uncomfortable. I've heard stories of teams completing the daily crossword from the newspaper, checking emails, regaling with tales from the weekend and engaging in unprofessional and personal commentary of staff members; the mind boggles, but without a clear purpose and direction, the meeting has no purpose.

When conducting professional learning teams (PLTs) or professional learning communities (PLCs), they are the kind of meetings that run well with an agenda or focused topic. When conducting these, either give some broad brushstrokes as to the direction or really detailed items that would be analysed, discussed or covered.

Imagine. You. Just. Stopped. Stopped talking. Stopped planning. Stopped being the person at the front of the room in charge of the learning. Imagine you said to your students, it is over to you now – go for it. Who knows what would happen – but we can imagine! Disengagement; engagement in anything other than learning; a handful of conscientious students would seize the opportunity with both hands; some would take a well-earned nap; and others would fit somewhere else in this chaotic wheel of colour. Sound anything like a meeting without an agenda?

Trust

"Trust I seek, and I find in you, every day for us something new, open mind for a different view and nothing else matters" – Metallica. But if Metallica isn't your cup of tea, perhaps John Hattie is, "We want students to trust their teachers and know what they are learning, why they are learning, and knowing their progress in their learning" (Hattie, 2023).

They both got this one right! Ponder for a moment: do I trust my students? That takes some think time and some real introspection of practice. A different and important way of looking at the concept of trust is: do your students trust you? If you are a leader, replace the word students with teachers/staff in the previous statements and see how that sits with you. Why not be explicit and seek staff feedback on this as to how you are trusted? Find a way to make things anonymous and get a real insight as to how your trust is perceived.

Focusing on the students again, how do we develop trust with them? There are times when we, as teachers, need to embody what it is we want in students. We need to be genuine and consistent. If we want our students to be risktakers in their learning, we need to model that. Students understand when we say we want to see something or for them to be something, but if we aren't that ourselves, then we are sending mixed messages.

Develop genuine learning relationships with students and get to know them as individuals. Notice haircuts, ask them how their game was on the weekend, notice if they mention an event coming up and inquire as to how it was. Take those 30 seconds in the morning when they are coming in and unpacking their bags to invest in getting to know them. During the day, get to know them as learners, too. Not what they are learning and struggling with, but also what motivates them or engages them in their learning. Notice the opposite and see if you can't develop learning sequences that fit with their preferences.

Be honest and give feedback on learning or effort. If you acknowledge everyone's output as 'good job' or 'great effort', then you probably aren't acknowledging any of them fairly. Customise your feedback so that it is reflective of individuals. The student who ordinarily performs by achieving 95% in Maths and a student who normally achieves 37% have both put 100% effort in. You can equally reward their effort and praise them with appropriate feedback. But on the next day, if they both got 50% on their test, there is a significant drop for one and gain for the other. Your feedback needs to match that. There may well be a story underneath the normally higher performing student. Lead with questions and seek to understand.

Celebrating successes – big or small – is a great way to generate trust. If the students view you as genuinely invested in their progress and success, they will more than likely view you as someone who values and appreciates their efforts. It can also serve to reinforce positive behaviours and attitudes that you want to build in your classroom learning community. What a positive space it would be to have that as the norm. Imagine if it were not only you who celebrated their successes, but their fellow students. The trust from peer to peer would also flourish.

As a primary school teacher, you get to hear all kinds of responses to questions – from the sublime to the ridiculous and everything in between. How you respond to these will send signals to your students. If upon hearing a wonderful response, you shower that student with praise and point out how good the response was, you are indicating to the students that this is the kind of thinking you value in your class.

Heutagogy (hyoo-tuh-goh-jee)

Hase and Kenyon (2000) shared their findings on heutagogy as "the study of self-determined learning, may be viewed as a natural progression from earlier educational methodologies..." But what exactly is it?

In essence, heutagogy is self-directed learning by students that is supported by teachers who scaffold and guide learning. Differing from pedagogy (the method and practice of teaching) and andragogy (the method and practice of teaching adult learners), it is the method and practice of how students are empowered to take control of their learning and development. Its premise is that students have the capacity to be self-directed in their learning and that the teacher's role is that of support and guidance and allows for the students to take ownership of their learning.

Pedagogy, Andragogy and Heutagogy compared

	Pedagogy Children's learning	Andragogy Adults' learning	Heutagogy Self-directed learning
Dependence	The learner is a dependent personality. Teacher determines what, how and when anything is learned.	Adults are independent. They strive for autonomy and self-direction in learning.	Learners are interdependent. They identify the potential to learn from novel experiences as a matter of course. They are able to manage their own learning.
Resources for learning	The learner has few resources – the teacher devises transmission techniques to store knowledge in the learner's head.	Adults use their own and others' experience.	Teacher provides some resources, but the learner decides the path by negotiating the learning.
Reasons for learning	Learn in order to advance to the next stage.	Adults learn when they experience a need to know or perform more effectively.	Learning is not necessarily based on need but on the identification of the potential to learn in novel situations.
Focus of learning	Learning is subject-centred, focused on prescribed curriculum and planned sequences according to the logic of the subject matter.	Adult learning is task- or problem-centred.	Learners can go beyond problem solving by enabling proactivity. Learners use their own and others' experiences and internal processes such as reflection, environmental scanning, experience, interaction with others, and proactive as well as problem-solving behaviours.

Motivation	Motivation comes from external sources – usually parents, teachers and a sense of competition.	Motivation stems from internal sources – the increased self-esteem, confidence and recognition that come from successful performance.	Self-efficacy, knowing how to learn, creativity and the ability to use these qualities in novel as well as familiar situations and working with others.
Role of the teacher	Designs the learning process, imposes material, is assumed to know best.	Enabler or facilitator, climate or collaboration, respect and openness.	Develop the learner's capability. Capable people: • Know how to learn • Are creative • Have a high degree of self-efficacy • Apply competencies in the novel as well as familiar situations • Can work well with others.

www.teachthought.com/pedagogy/andragogy

The above table, created by Lindy McKeown Orwin, suggests that there is a developmental continuum of learners that needs to be progressed through. It dictates that students (children) need to learn how to be taught to learn, then progress to learning as an adult before they can take control of their own learning. Sugata Mitra's computer in a hole in a Delhi wall certainly suggests that children have the motivation and capacity to learn without adults supporting them. I know that when I play FIFA with my 13-year-old son, he has taught himself all manner of tricks and techniques that I haven't mastered (or even considered). That is because he plays more often, takes risks and tries things out. He has gone online and researched, asked his friends and learnt through practice. He has learnt experientially. Measuring him against the classifications on the above model, here's where he sits…

- **Dependence** – Heutagogy – He is self-directing and is beyond independent.

- **Resources for learning** – Heutagogy – The game and console were purchased, but that is where my resourcing stopped. He has sought out all the avenues for learning.
- **Reasons for learning** – Heutagogy – He has learnt things that he hasn't even done against me. He just learns in case one day he will need a trick or two.
- **Focus of learning** – Heutagogy – He has found a problem and identified how to go about solving it. The only problem now is I can't lay a glove on him in FIFA.
- **Motivation** – Heutagogy – Completely intrinsically motivated to do better and perform well.
- **Role of the teacher** – Heutagogy – He has become the teacher as he teaches me how to do some of the techniques and skills (but as we know, just because something is taught, doesn't mean it has been learnt).

Did he progress through all the stages of pedagogy in order to go through andragogy to arrive finally at heutagogy? I don't recall him entering adulthood. It is clear that he is operating at a level in this field completely autonomously and is self-directed. He didn't need to work through all the previous levels to arrive where he is. Similarly, there is a debate around comprehension – it has three levels (literal, inferential and evaluative). There is a body of work coming from Monash University that suggests these should be called types of comprehension and students can access all at any time. Is it possible the same case could be made for the three stages of 'agogy'?

Let's not assume that students can't.

Perhaps we should start with the mindset that students can. They can and are capable of doing many things – we just need to provide the necessary conditions to listen to their voice. Student voice doesn't have to be that the students are in total control of the learning at every stage. For some settings, this is not possible and for other settings, this is too far from their current reality to readily transition to.

Student voice can be on a spectrum. Nowhere is it written (or at least that I have discovered) there is a right and a wrong way of including student voice or a definitive preferred manner. Consider the possibility that there is a sliding scale of student voice – it has to work for your context. The ideal is to establish:

- Where you are
- How you can provide opportunities for student voice
- A plan of how to develop it more
- A way to refine how you currently do it

One simple way is by having three-way conferences. As mentioned previously, I liken having parent-teacher interviews without the student present to your annual review meeting with only your principal and your own parents. To be absented from the process is disempowering and suggests that those who are involved are important in these conversations. Include your students in these important meetings, as they are about their progress, their learning, their voice and their questions, and it builds trust. When doing this, it is so important to empower them and give them a purpose to being there and learn how to meaningfully contribute.

Chapter summary

- Student voice is worth listening to – students outnumber us in a classroom many times over.
- If you are going to ask the students their thoughts or wondering – be prepared to not be tokenistic – be genuine and provide time and space to factor these wonderings in.
- Review the roles the teacher and students play at different stages of an inquiry; they should not be the same through the stages of an inquiry.
- Audit how students are communicating their learning or choosing their final piece of action.
- Intentionally plan to allow time for student voice (or even better, include it in the planning).
- There is a lot of trust required for student voice in a classroom. Consider how your learning relationships are when viewed through the lens of trust.
- Heutagogy as a way to learn is introduced to encourage self-directed learning.
- Listen to their voice and listen often – take moments to intentionally find out their learning.
- Student voice can be on a spectrum – if we have the right instruments and focus, we can hear it.

Reflection

Explore how you capture moments of student voice.

Using the structure of KWLs...

- **What do you do with all the Ks the students provide?** Are they used in direct response when planning or do you 'average' out that there are certain things that don't need teaching and others that just are going to be?
- **What do you do with all the Ws?** Are these questions informing your planning or your capacity to support inquiries? Are they questions asked that go greatly unanswered?
- **What is the point of the L?** Are you filling it out? Do you even need to? Is there other learning that evidences this instead? Sometimes we forget about the filling in the L, but the learning (and the process to get there) is key. How do you capture the L?
- **When do you capture student voice?** You can capture student voice at any time, so long as you are listening.

CHAPTER 11

LIGHTS, CAMERA, ~~TEACHER-LED~~ ACTION

> *"A small group of thoughtful people could change the world.
> Indeed, it's the only thing that ever has"*
> **– Margaret Mead (1949)**

> *"I've got everything I need right here, between my hands and
> there it is right in front of me"*
> **– Chairlift: 'Ch-Ching'**

What really is action? Is there a difference between genuine action, teacher-led action, student-initiated action or planned action? How can we get our students to take action? If I am leading the students, is it truly action or an activity? Through this chapter, we will explore what action is and how the roles of students and teachers significantly impact whether it is action or activity.

This chapter is broken down into the following sections:

- Scenarios – action or activity?
- Hart's Ladder of Participation
- Developing a shared definition of action
- Time and space

Scenarios – action or activity?

Ponder the following examples and work out whether they are examples of action or activity.

Scenario 1

Our Grade 3 team was conducting an inquiry into the nature of national identity and what it means to be Australian. We knew at the time we wanted the students to do something positive with their learning and not just recognise what makes an Australian (and that is a highly complex and almost indefinable goal). In the background, as learning and teaching leader, I contacted the Department of Immigration and inquired about the possibility of hosting a citizenship ceremony at our school. They were more than happy for it to occur but asked that I liaise with the local council as they conduct them on behalf of the department. Through emails and phone calls, it was arranged that we would host a citizenship ceremony at our school at night. The students were so motivated and excited. The teachers put the students in charge of organising different elements, from staging, catering, ushering, invitations, order of speakers, seating, name tags, etc. Every aspect of the evening was coordinated by the students through the guiding hands of teachers.

This was the first instance of a citizenship ceremony being hosted by a school and we felt pretty proud. The students were beyond thrilled with the role they played and the new citizens equally thrilled by the ceremony and the student participation. As a school, it was great to have such visibility in the community, and it led to other councils reaching out to their local schools to see if they could offer the same.

But was it action?

Scenario 2

As a teaching team, we organised an incredible experience taking our Grade 5 and 6 students to a tertiary institution focused on fashion design. Our inquiry we were exploring was art as a form of expression and the design process. Clearly, we wanted the learning to go in the fashion design direction; if not, we would have organised different excursions to expose our students to different forms of art. We, as teachers, had in our minds that it would be amazing if we could organise a fashion show at school and invite the school community. The students worked so hard on their designs, invitations and set-up of the hall. The students documented their learning journeys digitally and were able to compose short films to share their learning. They created music and backgrounds for their 'fashion catwalks'. Families came along and it was a huge success, with so many acknowledgements of effort and process, design and innovation. It was a massive night of learning and demonstration of what was learnt, while demonstrating a vulnerability and confidence to share.

But was it action?

Scenario 3

In the last term of the year in Grade 5, we wanted to plan an inquiry that was going to have the capacity for the students to showcase their creativity while displaying their scientific knowledge of circuits and electricity. We set the inquiry up beautifully and took the students on an excursion to see the Myer Christmas Windows. For those unaware, these are an annual event in Melbourne where shop windows tell a story using lights, music and moving pieces. The idea was that we would take the students there, they would become inspired by what they saw and be able to create their own. Returning to school, we had successfully inspired the students to become engaged in storytelling and they were excited about telling a story using technology, electrical circuitry and creativity.

We then asked the students what would happen if we used our knowledge of storytelling, circuitry and social justice to create something for our school community and raise money for those in need at Christmas? They were pretty keen to do something with their knowledge. They came up with the idea of creating a localised version of the Christmas windows that parents could attend with the idea of making a donation to a charity while visiting the school for Christmas carols.

The students raised money for their charity, the parents were so moved and impressed, and the learning was on display.

But was it action?

Scenario 4

Starting off an inquiry focusing on sustainability and environmentalism, we thought it would be a great idea to play the clip 'Dear Future Generations: Sorry' by Prince Ea (www.youtube.com/watch?v=eRLJscAlk1M). This was used to stimulate the students into thinking 'We need to do something to make the world a better place!' We developed a plan to continue to stimulate the students and provoke their thinking through many other means.

Eventually, as we needed to cover energy usage (curriculum accountability through curriculum mapping), we introduced the various ways we, as humans, produce and consume energy. The teaching phase of the unit culminated with the question: *How could you use your knowledge of sustainability to design information to share about your chosen energy issue?*

But was this action?

The answer to each of the four scenarios depends on your definition of action. So, how do you define action? Is it a matter of students doing something with their learning at the end of an inquiry? Is it the final demonstration of knowledge and understanding in the form chosen by a student to complete the inquiry? Or something entirely different again?

Hart's Ladder of Participation

Consider the writings of Roger Hart (2003), in his piece where he says, "The highest possible degree of citizenship in my view is when we, children or adults, not only feel that we can initiate some change ourselves but when we also recognise that it is sometimes appropriate to also invite others to join us because of their own rights and because it affects them too, as fellow-citizens."

Does your definition of action include change? Ultimately, we should want student actions to change something. Simply, action can be viewed as changing their own or the life of another. In light of that, all the previous scenarios are indeed changing their own or others' lives, but let's get a little more sophisticated around the conditions that create action.

The stage of Hart's Ladder of Participation are:

1. Manipulation
2. Decoration
3. Tokenism
4. Assigned but informed
5. Consulted and informed
6. Adult-initiated shared decisions with children
7. Child-initiated and directed
8. Child-initiated shared decisions with adults

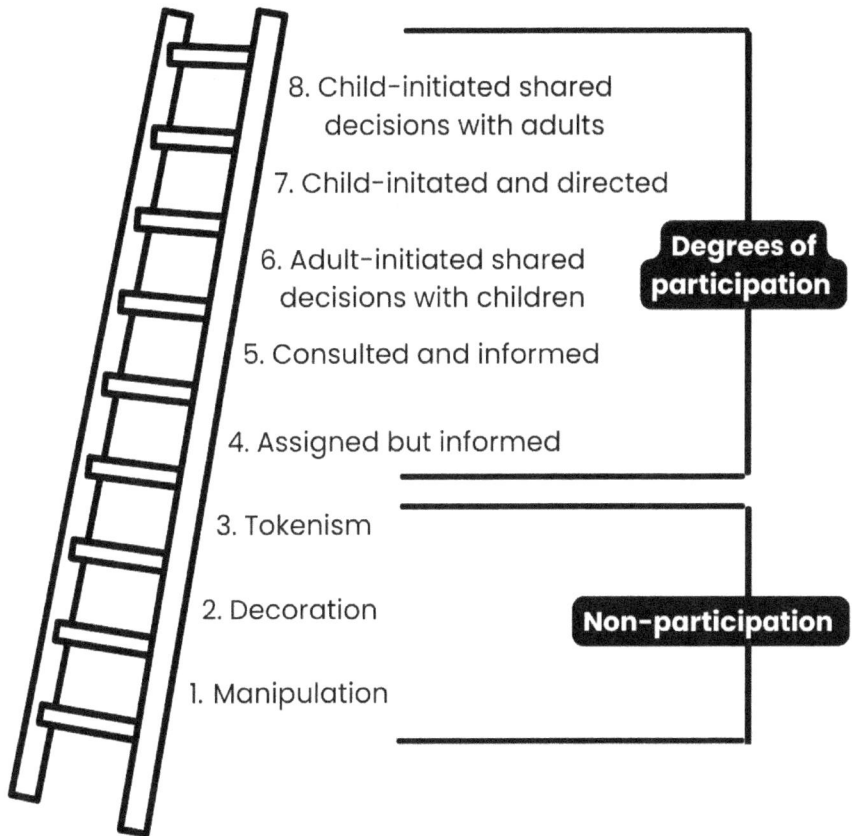

The Ladder of Participation

The first three rungs (manipulation, decoration and tokenism) are classified as non-participation (not true participation), whereas the next five describe the degree or level of true participation.

1. **Manipulation** – is where adults use children to support causes and 'pretend' that the causes are inspired by children. Think of when you see children holding up signs at a protest rally; they are doing so because their parents told them to.
2. **Decoration** – is where young people are used to help or bolster a cause in a relatively indirect way, although adults do not pretend that the cause is inspired by children. This is when you may see children holding gifts or flowers to visiting dignitaries, regents or politicians.
3. **Tokenism** – is where young people appear to be given a voice but in fact have little or no choice about what they do or how they participate!

Think of your average school assembly. The teacher wants the class to perform due to their teacher/class already being rostered on, but the assembly is out of the students' control. The performance/prayer/items are chosen by the teacher, students are given roles and are essentially told they are performing.

4. **Assigned but informed** – is where children are assigned a specific role and informed about how and why they are being involved. Using the same example of the assembly, the teacher wants the class to perform or lead the assembly, but the difference is they tell them why. The 'performance' is still chosen by the teacher, roles are still assigned and the students are still told they are performing. The important difference to acknowledge is the students are informed about how and why they are involved, however, they are not in control.

5. **Consulted and informed** – is where children give advice on projects or programs designed and run by adults. Children are informed about how their input will be used, however, the decisions are made by adults. In this scenario, the teacher still tells the students they are performing, tells them why, the roles are decided by the teacher, but the key difference is the content. This time, the students have the choice as to what they 'perform'.

6. **Adult-initiated shared decisions with children** – is where projects or programs are initiated by adults, but the decision-making is shared with young people. This time, the assembly is still decided upon by the teacher and the students are informed why – but now the students have a great deal more scope and decision-making power. The students decide what is to be performed, who will be performing what role, what needs to be done and there is a sense of 'buy-in', with students actively wanting to participate.

7. **Child-initiated and directed** – is where young people initiate and direct a project or program. Adults are involved only in a supportive role. Moving away from adult-centred decision-making and the real shift of ownership is this next step. The students are passionate about their learning and wish to perform at an assembly. They are in charge of deciding the roles and the content for the performance. The teacher's role is purely administrative. They may need to photocopy certain scripts or readings and liaise with administration to organise the allocation of the assembly.

8. **Child-initiated shared decisions with adults** – is where projects or programs are initiated by children and decision-making is shared among children and adults. These projects empower children while at the same time enable them to access and learn from the life experiences and expertise of adults. It is similar to the above scenario, but there is even greater scope for student ownership. The students decide to perform at the assembly, decide on the focus/content and allocate the roles. However, this time, the students seek to use the expertise or input of the teacher for guidance on which performance or focus and which students would be best for each role. The teacher's input is consultative and only suggestive, not definitive.

These are the different levels that student action can occur. We need to ensure that it is an action that takes place, not a teacher-led activity or predetermined task. With further thinking around what action is, everyone on your staff will have a different nuanced version of it. Action is about the active engagement and participation of students in their learning process. It goes beyond passively listening to the teacher and the non-participative stages of Hart's Ladder of Participation. It is a way to encourage students to apply their learning through taking control and exercising voice, choice and ownership – some real agency. In order to ensure there is a consistency of knowledge and articulation, an exercise to narrow the definition needs to take place.

Developing a shared definition of action

A powerful way to develop a shared understanding or consistency of belief is to engage in an activity called 'Thinking Trade'. This is best done with all the staff you need to ensure all are on the same page – my advice would be all teaching staff, but you may wish to include all staff, or at a broader level (at a different time), involve the students as well.

If you are working with staff, have them seated at tables in groups of around four to six. Any more than that and there is potential for big voices to dominate and for important or possible ideas to not be voiced or listened to. You may wish to be selective in how you group your staff, ranging from natural teams, random allocation, representation of teams in each group or any other method you prefer.

Here's what to do:

1. Provide each participant with five Post-it notes.
2. Ask each participant to record a word (or two words maximum) on each Post-it note that are important when it comes to action.
3. Inform the participant that they are about to trade some words with other members of staff.
4. Instruct the participants to leave their two most important (or favourite) Post-it notes at their seat/table.
5. Invite staff to walk around the room with their other three Post-it notes and trade them with someone else.
   a. They can't swap more than one Post-it note with any one person.
   b. They can't swap for the exact word they have back at their seat/table.
   c. They can't swap for the exact word they already have in their hand.
   d. They can't return until they have swapped all three.

Now the participants can return to their original seats/tables and review their new set of five words. With their table the task now is to aggregate as many ideas as possible in order to streamline the thinking and development of the next phase. As you are working with Post-it notes, they can be placed on the table in groups and easily moved if need be. Invite the teams to group the words together – this simple process ensures that individual voices are not heard, it is purely a process of identification and alignment.

Now that teams/tables have aggregated their thinking, the next task is to get them to use the words (ideally, the words that came up more frequently will dominate the thinking) and develop a sentence that defines what action is to them. This part will take a little time as there are personalities, preconceived notions and preferences involved. Ensure that you instruct the teams to develop them using the words in front of them. You may wish to enforce that the three most frequently used words have to be used explicitly in their sentence or other such criterion.

While teams are engaging in this task, it is advantageous for someone to roam the room and listen in to the different conversations. It may help gain an insight into the thinking of individuals or potential moments to redirect thinking if they are not 'complying' with the protocols of the exercise.

You may get teams that ask for sentences rather than singular words. It is entirely up to you how you wish to proceed. If the thinking is impeded by limiting it to one sentence, then change the conditions and allow it. Once all groups have developed their sentence(s), have them read them out to the room. There will be some moments when one table or team nails it and there is an audible appreciation of their wording. Your role in conducting this isn't to validate any team's work over another, simply thank them for their contribution and move on to the next one.

After each team has contributed their sentence(s), invite feedback or commentary from the participants – it may come in the form of which they liked or disliked, which resonated with them or what they were challenged by.

You could conduct a compass point activity exploring the following:

- **N – New** – What was new for you?
- **E – Excites** – What excites you?
- **W – Worries** – What are some worries you have?
- **S – Suggestions** – What are some suggestions you may have?

With teams thinking in these ways, they will begin to critique, more formally, the thinking of others and that of their own. Ask teams to see if, after listening and reflecting on others' sentences, they want to refine and 'publish' their sentence. Provide them with a large piece of butcher's paper in order for it to be displayed. I love when teachers work on these and the final one on display has all the hallmarks of heavily edited work and thinking. It needn't be the polished final product that is displayed, but the more organic and revised ones that represent the cognitive journey of the team. If you want the process finished while everyone is present and in the headspace for it, provide each participant with a star or sticker to place votes on the one that resonates the most with them. Depending on the spread of results, you may wish to start to cull the lesser voted for and re-vote based on the top three (or two) or suggest merging some of the sentences together. However you do it, it should be collaborative and not directive in the final product.

You may wish to let this sit with the staff and display them in a public/shared space where staff can consider them or provide written feedback on them. If you do this, then there needs to be a time limit on how long you are going to leave them up. You may wish to write them up and send them out as a survey to seek staff input and have them vote. Or you could seek a working party to take the thinking from the room on the day to create a final statement that encapsulates the thinking of the room. It would be prudent to seek the input of a range of staff rather than just leadership as this can tend to be seen as 'we've done all that work and they just go away and write what they wanted'.

Once it is finalised, you need to share it – share it with the staff, share it with any members of staff who weren't there, share it with parents via the newsletter, share it with the board or parent committee, share it on your website so everyone can see that you not only value action, but what it means to your school. But, above all, share it with the students. Your actions can serve as a catalyst for action and participation. They are the ones who will be taking it and they need to know what it is or isn't and how you define it and will be looking for.

Time and space

Traditionally, when we as teachers plan, we plan out the entire inquiry or learning sequences and design that final action. Think of the scenarios from earlier in this chapter – they were predominantly teacher-led and the students were participating in them, but ultimately, I wouldn't classify all of them as action, as they were not student-directed or initiated. Which leads to the questions of:

- Do students need to take action?
- What happens if I leave time and space and they don't take action?
- How will I fit all my teaching in?

Starting with the last question, the work of Wiggins and McTighe (2005) in *Understanding by Design* should help to support teachers in the struggle to 'fit everything in'.

Understanding by Design: Stages of Backward Design
(Wiggins & McTighe, 2005)

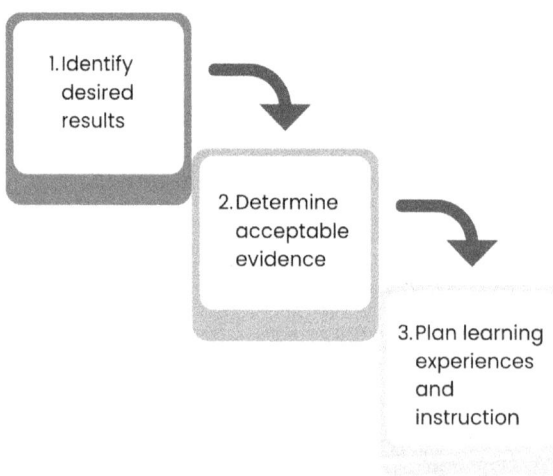

Step 1. Consider your desired results to be curriculum coverage and understanding or knowledge of the content that the inquiry is intended to cover. This should be from your mapped curriculum and the statement and mini inquiries. This is, after all, what you want the students to learn.

Step 2 asks the teacher to work out the ways they can find out if students have reached desired results. Are there certain assessments or indicators along the way that you can plan for or design to capture their learning?

Step 3 is to set about the explicitness of teaching or planning the learning experiences. It calls on the teacher to consider the resources and materials required along with thinking about what skills and knowledge the students will need to succeed. It also calls upon teachers to plan learning experiences that will support student learning.

When you consider the above three-step process, overlay that with the timeline of the inquiry. If the inquiry is allocated for a seven-week block, then consider how long your time teaching and delivering learning experiences will be. If you have enough for seven weeks, then you will never genuinely provide time and space for student action. Ask the question: how long could the students need to take action? This shift in leaving time and space at the end of an inquiry may not be pure and organic like a student spontaneously taking action, but it is significantly better than not leaving the time or space. Leaving time for action (student initiated) is no different to leaving space for teacher-led action in terms of time. It is our purpose, expectations and the roles we play in this space that ultimately defines it as action or activity.

Now consider that your desired results are that the students should take action about the topic. You follow the three steps from Wiggins and McTighe and you end up with the scenario that you simply can't make students take action. And you can't. Making students take action is simply a teacher-led activity. Students need to be led through and challenged, provoked and engaged enough in the content, issue or topic (inquiry) for them to want to engage in a response.

Now consider that your desired results are attitudinal, and you want the students to feel something about some content or issue. This is not to be confused with feeling a certain way about a topic. You would go through the same following two steps of the process, but the answers would be entirely different. If you have ensured that your instructional time or planned learning experiences are allocated for a certain period of time and that there is still time remaining in the inquiry, students have time, space and desire to take action.

We've all heard the saying 'You can lead a horse to water, but you can't make it drink'. What we are attempting to do here is provide a sense of thirst for the students – a thirst for action and further knowledge, doing something meaningful with their learning and not just 'playing school'. But even more powerful than leading the students, we simply provide a pathway to where there may be water. Present a landscape that has watering holes evident – some close, easy to achieve, some further away and a struggle to achieve, and others may well be hidden that no one knew about until someone started digging.

Action in the classroom helps foster active, engaged and empowered learners. It helps students develop skills, attitudes and values that will serve them well beyond their primary school years.

Students will, determined by their experiences, knowledge, skills, desires and passions, engage in inquiries differently. Some will be totally engaged in one inquiry and approach with a sense of ambivalence to the next. We need to find what works for these students – each and every single one of them. Provide rich and rewarding learning opportunities. Have students engage in learning that challenges their minds, their preconceived notions and makes them want to take action and make a difference. Ultimately, we need to model all the things we want our students to be – and one of the biggest is being passionate about learning.

We can't teach passion, but we can teach with it.

Chapter summary

- Students are all capable of taking action – if only we provide the time, space and capacity to listen.
- There is a difference between an activity and action.
- Hart's Ladder of Participation provides the opportunity to explore how the different levels of student participation can look.
- There are many different types of action and it is imperative that schools decide on what action looks like in their setting.
- Thinking Trade as a strategy for consensus and team thinking is powerful and used for a definition of action.
- Questions are asked about whether students indeed have to take action.
- Exploration of Backward Design demonstrates how student action can look in a classroom.

Reflection

Evaluate your last inquiry's element of action.

Was it any of the following:

- Manipulation
- Decoration
- Tokenism
- Assigned but informed
- Consulted and informed
- Adult-initiated shared decisions with children
- Child-initiated and directed
- Child-initiated shared decisions with adults

If it was anything but the last two rungs on the ladder (child-initiated and directed or child-initiated shared decisions with adults), consider the following:

- What level did the students achieve?
- Is this what I was aiming for?
- What did I do to help my students achieve the level they did?
- What did I do to stop my students from reaching these levels?
- What skills do I need to share with my students to allow them to achieve the higher levels?

If it was either child-initiated and directed or child-initiated shared decisions with adults), consider the following:

- What level did the students achieve?
- Is this what I was aiming for?
- What did I do to help my students achieve the level they did?
- What did I do to stop my students from reaching these levels?
- What skills do I need to share with my students to allow them to achieve the higher levels?
- What can I take away from this inquiry to make sure I achieve these levels again?

At what stage of the inquiry did the action come?

- Was it planned or planned for?
- Did it come at the end of the inquiry?
- Did it come at the end of your 'teaching'?
- Was it organic and occurred when the students took action?

CONCLUSION

FINAL THOUGHTS

"Progress is impossible without change, and those who cannot change their minds cannot change anything"
– **George Bernard Shaw (1945)**

"The gold road's sure a long road. Winds on through the hill for fifteen days"
– **The Stone Roses: 'Fools Gold'**

I hope after reading this you feel as though you are better placed to become the teacher you aspire to be. There are no shortcuts to success; if there were, we would have, through research and meta-analyses, discovered them already. The levels of cognition, time and effort cannot be understated. We can't magic up structures or skills, we need to intentionally plan for them and/or create them.

Inquiry is a lot of fun and it should be. Learning is a lot of fun and it should be. Schools should be joyful places and we need to ensure that we provide our teachers with the skills and time to develop their craft in inquiry learning in order for the students to develop theirs. The structures and processes outlined in this book are the investment in order for learning and teaching to flourish.

These are our bamboo moments.

Bamboo is fast growing once it breaks through the soil, but it takes time and constant care in order to reach that stage. This is the nurturing and creation of structures.

Growing bamboo is much like inquiry-based learning – the focus is on the process, not the end result. Simply harvesting bamboo as it shoots through doesn't demonstrate the full flourishing of the plant. This is when we allow students to ask questions and develop their inquiries instead of charging ahead ignoring their wonderings.

Bamboo and inquiry-based learning both require flexibility and adaptation. The weather and environment are constantly changing and there are also the growing conditions. This is our ability as educators to pivot and change and be agile in how we respond to student interests or wonderings.

Bamboo offers long-term benefits. Bamboo is a sustainable resource for building materials, foods and other resources that will never be seen in the setting where they are grown. Similarly, inquiry-based learning offers sustainable long-term learning skills and dispositions. These are the skills and approaches to learning we want to develop and foster in our students, so when they leave our schools, secondary schools and universities, they enter the world outside of education with confidence, wonder and awe.

"You can paint these wings and make them fly"
– Låpsley: '**Painter (Valentine)**'

REFERENCES

Australian Institute for Teaching and School Leadership (AITSL) (2017). 'Australian Professional Standards for Teachers.' Retrieved February 2023, from www.aitsl.edu.au/standards

Bybee, RW (1997). *Achieving scientific literacy: From purposes to practices.* Portsmouth, NH: Heinemann.

Department for Education (United Kingdom) (2011). 'Teachers Standards: Guidance for school leavers, school staff and governing bodies.' Retrieved February 2023, from assets.publishing.service.gov.uk/government/uploads/system/uploads/attachment_data/file/1040274/Teachers__Standards_Dec_2021.pdf

Department of Education, Australian Government (2014). *Review of the Australian Curriculum – Initial Australian Government Response.* www.education.gov.au/download/2439/review-australian-curriculum-initial-australian-government-response/18271/document/docx

Dewey, J (1933). *How we think: A restatement of the relation of reflective thinking to the educative process.* Boston, MA: DC Heath.

Drucker, PF, Kuhl, JS, & Hesselbein, F (2015). *Peter Drucker's Five Most Important Questions: Enduring Wisdom for Today's Leaders.* John Wiley & Sons.

Education International & UNESCO (2019). *Global Framework of Professional Teaching Standards.* Retrieved February 2023, from www.ei-ie.org/en/item/25734:global-framework-of-professional-teaching-standards

Erickson, HL (2001). *Stirring the Head, Heart, and Soul: Redefining Curriculum and Instruction.* (Second edition.) Corwin Press.

Gambetti, A (April 2015). Reggio Emilia.

Gardner, H (1989). *The Unschooled Mind: How Children Think and How Schools Should Teach.* New York: Basic Books.

Goff, B (2014). *Love Does.* Nashville, TN: Thomas Nelson.

Harden, RM (2001). 'AMEE Guide No. 21: Curriculum mapping: a tool for transparent and authentic teaching and learning.' *Medical Teacher.* 2001;23:123–137.

Harpaz, Y (2005). 'Teaching and learning in a community of thinking.' *Journal of Curriculum and Supervision.* 20(2), 136–157.

Harpaz, Y (2007). 'Approaches to Teaching Thinking: Toward a Conceptual Mapping of the Field.' Teachers College Record: The Voice of Scholarship in Education. 109(8), 1845–1874. doi:10.1177/016146810710900801.

Hart, RA (2003). *Children's Participation: From Tokenism to Citizenship.* New York: UNICEF.

Hart, R (n.d.). 'Ladder of Children's Participation.' Retrieved May 2023, from https://organizingengagement.org/models/ladder-of-childrens-participation

Hase, S, & Kenyon, C (2000). 'From andragogy to heutagogy.' Ultibase Articles. 5. 1–10.

Hattie, J (2009). *Visible Learning: A Synthesis of Over 800 Meta-Analyses Relating to Achievement.* London, UK: Routledge.

Hattie, J (2023). *Visible Learning: The Sequel – A Synthesis of Over 2,100 Meta-Analyses Relating to Achievement.* London, UK: Routledge.

Heick, T (2015). 'The Difference Between Pedagogy, Andragogy, and Heutagogy.' TeachThought. Retrieved May 2023, from www.teachthought.com/pedagogy/andragogy

Hunter, J, Haywood, A, & Parkinson, N (2022). *Ending the lesson lottery: How to improve curriculum planning in schools.* Grattan Institute.

Kuhlthau, CC, Maniotes, LK, & Caspari, AK (2007). *Guided Inquiry: Learning in the 21st century.* Westport, CN: Libraries Unlimited.

Marzano, RJ, & Kendall, JS (2007). *The New Taxonomy of Educational Objectives.* A review of the book by Marzano, R, & Schwille, J. Bloomington, IN: Solution Tree Press.

McGlone, F, & Walker, S (2021). 'Four health benefits of hugs – and why they feel so good.' The Conversation. Retrieved May 2023, from www.theconversation.com/four-health-benefits-of-hugs-and-why-they-feel-so-good-160935

McKinlay, M, & Ottley, M (2020). *How to make a Bird.* Newtown, NSW: Walker Books Australia Pty Ltd.

Mead, M (1949). *Male and female: a study of the sexes in a changing world.* New York: Morrow.

Murdoch, K (2021). 'Curiosity, courage and the field beyond.' Retrieved April 2023, from www.kathmurdoch.com.au/blog/2021/4/6/curiosity-courage-and-the-field-beyond#:~:text=Inquiry%20is%20not%20about%20getting,arrive%20at%20an%20unexpected%20destination

Murdoch, K, & Claxton, G (2015). *The Power of Inquiry.* Northcote: Seastar Education.

National Board for Professional Teaching Standards (1989). 'Five Core Propositions.' Retrieved February 2023, from www.nbpts.org/certification/five-core-propostions

National Portal of India (2010). National Curriculum Framework. Retrieved February 2023, from www.india.gov.in/spotlight/national-curriculum-framework-ncf

Pedaste, M, Mäeots, M, Siiman, LA, De Jong, T, Van Riesen, SA, Kamp, ET, Manoli, CC, Zacharia, ZC, & Tsourlidaki, E (2015). 'Phases of inquiry-based learning: Definitions and the inquiry cycle.' *Educational Research Review*, 14, 47–61.

Project Zero (n.d.). 'Chalk Talk.' Harvard Graduate School of Education. Retrieved March 2023, from https://pz.harvard.edu/sites/default/files/Chalk%20Talk_1.pdf

Queensland Curriculum & Assessment Authority (n.d.). 'Categories of common cognitive verbs.' Retrieved April 2023, from www.qcaa.qld.edu.au/downloads/p_10/ac_categories_cognitive_verbs.pdf

Ritchhart, R, Church, M, & Morrison, K (2011). *Making Thinking Visible: How to Promote Engagement, Understanding, and Independence for All Learners.* San Francisco, CA: Jossey-Bass.

Robinson, K (2006). 'Do schools kill creativity?' TED Talk. Retrieved April 2023, from www.ted.com/talks/sir_ken_robinson_do_schools_kill_creativity

Rudduck, J (2007). 'Student Voice, Student Engagement, and School Reform.' In Thiessen, D, & Cook-Sather, A (Eds.), *International Handbook of Student Experience in Elementary and Secondary School* (pp. 587–610). Dordrecht, Netherlands: Springer.

Shaw, GB (1945). *Everybody's Political What's What?* Constable.

Short, KG (2009). *Inquiry as a stance on curriculum.* In Barratt, L, Barrett, MB, & Northcote, MS (Eds.), *Taking the PYP Forward* (43–59). International Baccalaureate Organization. Retrieved September 2023 from www.ibmidatlantic.org/Inquiry_as_stance.pdf

Spencer, J, & Juliani, AJ (2017). *Empower: What Happens When Students Own Their Learning.* Columbia SC: IMPress Books.

Sweller, J, Ayres, P, Kalyuga, S, Sweller, J, Ayres, P, & Kalyuga, S (2011). *Measuring cognitive load. Cognitive load theory*, 71–85.

Thiessen, D, & Cook-Sather, A (2006). *International Handbook of Student Experience in Elementary and Secondary School.* Springer.

Tomlinson, CA, & Allan, SD (2000). *Leadership for Differentiating Schools & Classrooms.* Alexandria, VA: Association for Supervision and Curriculum Development.

United Nations, Department of Economic and Social Affairs (2022). 'Sustainable Development Goals: 4.' Retrieved February 2023, from https://sdgs.un.org/goals/goal4

Walsh, C (2020). 'What the nose knows.' *The Harvard Gazette.* Retrieved May 2023, from www.news.harvard.edu/gazette/story/2020/02/how-scent-emotion-and-memory-are-intertwined-and-exploited

Ward, WA (1968). *Thoughts of a Christian Optimist: The Words of William Arthur Ward.* Anderson, SC: Droke House; distributed by Grosset and Dunlap, New York.

Wiggins, G, & McTighe, J (2005). *Understanding by Design.* (Expanded Second Edition.) Alexandria, VA: Association for Supervision and Curriculum Development.

Williams, M, & Penman, D (2011). *Mindfulness: A practical guide to finding eace in a frantic world.* Piatkus, London.

ABOUT THE AUTHOR

Grant Lewis works as an educational consultant who focuses on curriculum design, inquiry learning, and teaches writing and advocating for student agency and staff development. He has worked as an educational leader for more than 20 years both in Australia and internationally across multiple primary schools. His work in designing curriculums that meets learners' needs is at the centre of his work ambitions.

www.ingramcontent.com/pod-product-compliance
Lightning Source LLC
Chambersburg PA
CBHW052132110526
44591CB00012B/1691